# FALLACY BOOK
## BOOT CAMP FOR YOUR BRAIN

STEP-BY-STEP WRITING / CRITICAL THINKING EXERCISES

Gary Pollitt
California State University, Fullerton

Craig Baker
California State University, Fullerton

# ATTACK THE TEXT PUBLISHING

**Fallacy Book: Boot Camp for Your Brain**
Copyright © 2006, by Attack The Text Publishing

Printed in the United States of America
ISBN 0-9755923-1-9

Attack The Text Publishing
1519 E. Chapman Ave #3000, Fullerton, CA. 92831
Phone & Fax: 760.488.5098
www.attackthetext.com

# CONTENTS

# Arguments

An ARGUMENT is a group of statements designed to persuade others to believe something is true.

Arguments have the following structure:

PREMISE + CONCLUSION = ARGUMENT

The PREMISE of an argument is a statement (or group of statements) put forth as *evidence* for accepting the conclusion.

The CONCLUSION of an argument is a statement that has at least one other statement (premise) in support of it. The conclusion is usually the main point the person is trying to make. A single statement by itself is not an argument. A statement by itself is merely an opinion or a position on some issue.

Consider the following statement:

**Students should be allowed to spend more time playing video games.**

This statement is mere opinion because the speaker does not give reasons why students should be allowed to spend more time playing video games.

Consider the following ARGUMENT:

**Students should be allowed to spend more time playing video games because it improves hand-eye coordination.**

This statement is an argument because there is one main point or conclusion (students should be allowed to spend more time playing video games) supported by at least one other statement or premise (playing video games improves hand-eye coordination). At least one premise is required to form an argument; however some arguments will have more than one premise.

When trying to identify arguments, identify the conclusion first and then ask what reasons the person gives to support the conclusion.

# Fallacies

A FALLACY is an error in reasoning. Fallacies can appear in written text or in spoken language.

Fallacies have the following structure:

FAULTY PREMISE(S) + CONCLUSION = FALLACY

In this book, you will write paragraphs responding to the following six fallacies.

## ABUSIVE AD HOMINEM

An abusive ad hominem fallacy is an abusive attack on a person rather than the issue being argued.

## EITHER / OR FALLACY

The either / or fallacy is the idea that only two alternatives exist when there are more and that one of the two alternatives is true or more favorable.

## FALSE ANALOGY

A false analogy fallacy is the belief that because two things are alike in some way they are alike in others.

## HASTY GENERALIZATION

The hasty generalization fallacy is a general statement based on an insufficient piece of evidence.

## NON SEQUITUR

A non sequitur fallacy has a conclusion that does not follow logically from a premise that supposedly supports it.

## POST HOC

The post hoc fallacy is the assumption that because one event happened before another event that the first event caused the second event.

# PART 1
# BUILDING FALLACIES

# Abusive Ad Hominem (argument to the person)

An ad hominem fallacy is an attack on a person rather than the issue being argued.

**My grand daughter Big Willa couldn't even keep a job at Bad Burger, so her thoughts on quantum physics and string theory have little value.**

The issue is physics; however, Big Willa's grandmother makes a personal attack on Willa and not the issue. The fact that Willa cannot hold a job at Bad Burger does not invalidate her argument.

Directions: fill in the blanks to complete the fallacy.

1. You're going to listen to Flannery's advice about working out? Don't you know that

   she can only bench press _____ pounds?
   *(Attack her weight lifting prowess.)*

2. My new college baseball coach was a second stringer in high school and throws like a

   soccer player. Therefore, we should not listen to his advice about _____.

3  Flaubert says I should clean my _____, but that lazy

   bum wants to lie around all day and watch interior design shows on the cable TV!

4. Mr. Milton says that I should _____

   What does he know? He _____.
   *(Attack Mr. Milton.)*

5. How can you say _____,

   when you _____?
   *(Attack the person.)*

# Either / Or Fallacy (false alternatives)

The either / or fallacy is the idea that only two alternatives exist and that one of the two alternatives is more favorable.

**Listen, punk; either give me your lunch money or plan on getting beat up after school!**

There are only two options offered: give into the bully's intimidation or face violence; however, other options exist: the "punk" could keep the money and tell someone he is being coerced, or he could keep the money and run away.

<u>Directions</u>: fill in the blanks.

1. My way or _____

2. America: either love it or _____

3. Either you buy me a new _____ or you do not love me! 🗙

4. Either I _____ or no one will like me.

5. Either you eat your broccoli or _____ 🗙

6. Either _____

    or _____

7. Either _____

    or _____

8. Either _____

    or _____

# False Analogy

A false analogy fallacy is the belief that because two things are alike in some ways they are alike in others.

**Going to school is like going to prison. People are always telling you what to do.**

School and prison are alike in that both students and prisoners receive instructions from teachers and guards. School, however, is for learning. The result of an education is more power and control for the student; prison is for punishing and controlling people who cannot handle the responsibility of freedom. In this way the two places are quite different.

Directions: fill in the blanks.

1. Being homeless is like being on an extended camping _____. You

   get to _____ under the stars and experience the joy of roughing it.

2. Paying taxes is like _____. You hand over your

   hard-earned money to criminals against your will!

3. If my teacher Mr. Spear doesn't do any homework, then I _____

   _____

4. Smoking in public is like _____

   because _____

5. If _____

   then _____

# Hasty Generalization (insufficient sample)

The hasty generalization fallacy is a generalization based on an inadequate piece of evidence.

**All politicians are crooks! Mayor Skinny Grossman of Ludville was found guilty of taking bribes, and as a small boy he stole money from the donation tray in church!**

The fact that Mayor Grossman is a crook is an inadequate piece of evidence to prove the crookedness of all politicians. He is just one man, albeit a bad one.

Directions: fill in the blanks.

1. People from my hometown are terrible dressers. Just look at _____ silly clothes.

2. Whales are not dangerous. _____

    _____
    *(Give an example of a safe encounter with a whale.)*

3. All guys are slobs. My ex boyfriend couldn't even clean his own _____

4. My grandma Beanbarf smoked cigarettes, and she lived until she was 102 years old!

    _____
    *(Make a generalization about cigarettes based on the above evidence.)*

5. Jim was left-handed, and he was clumsy. _____

    _____
    *(Make a generalization based on the preceding piece of insufficient evidence.)*

# Non Sequitur (does not follow)

A non sequitur fallacy is a conclusion that does not follow logically from an idea that supposedly supports it.

**Mike loves the snow. Let's bean him with snowballs!**

It does not follow logically that because Mike loves snow that someone should throw snowballs at him. Anyone who's ever been hit hard with a snowball knows it is not always a pleasant thing. Being hit with a snowball has less to do with snow and more to do with pain.

Directions: fill in the blanks.

1. Yip-yip is a good skater; therefore he must be a _____ student.
   *(Write a conclusion that does not logically follow from the premise.)*

2. Young Grendel does a lot of rap singing; he must be _____
   *(Write a conclusion that does not logically follow from the premise.)*

3. I did a lot of work in Mr. Plato's philosophy class, so I deserve an _____
   *(Write a conclusion that does not logically follow from the premise.)*

4. Tina got an 'A' on her math test. _____

   _____
   *(Write a conclusion that does not logically follow from the premise.)*

5. We are having a lot of problems in our marriage.

   I think that we should _____
   *(Write a conclusion that does not logically follow from the premise.)*

# Post Hoc (false cause)

The post hoc fallacy is the assumption that because one event happened before another event that the first event caused the second event.

**I know I'm allergic to you. After you walked into the room, I got a nasty rash!**

Just because the entrance into a room [event A] precedes the appearance of a nasty rash [event B] does not mean that entering the room caused the rash. Many factors could have contributed to the outbreak.

Directions: fill in the blanks.

1. I am convinced that yelling at my students is the key to good teaching. Before the

   mid-term I screamed at the little 'twits' and they all got _____ on their tests.

2. Last night the moon was full and Jon-Jon went crazy. _____

   _____

   *(Write a conclusion based on the belief that the first event caused the second event.)*

3. Ever since Rudi Galgudi moved in across the street, bad things have been happening in

   the neighborhood. _____
   *(Write a conclusion based on the belief that the first event caused the second event.)*

4. Of course this jellybean gives me good luck. You want proof? I stuck it up my nose

   yesterday and today _____
   *(Write a conclusion based on the belief that the first event caused the second event.)*

5. Cowboy Billy ate some soy protein and he died. That goes to prove that

   _____

   *(Write a conclusion based on the belief that the first event caused the second event.)*

# PART 2
# STANDARD FORM

# Standard Form

An argument can be easily analyzed when the part (premises and conclusion) are put into standard form. Therefore, the first step when analyzing arguments is to construct the argument in standard form.

The basic organization of standard is

Since (premise) _____ ,

Therefore (conclusion) _____ .


## EXAMPLE 1

ARGUMENT:     **"Mike loves the snow. Let's bean him with snowballs."**


Argument reconstructed into standard form.


Since (premise) ___Mike loves the snow,_____

Therefore (conclusion) ___he should be hit with a snowball._____


## EXAMPLE 2

ARGUMENT:     **"All politicians are crooks! Mayor Skinny Grossman of Ludville was found guilty of taking bribes, and as a boy he stole money from the donation tray in church!"**


Argument reconstructed into standard form.


Since (premise) ___Mayor Skinny Grossman is a crook,_____

Therefore (conclusion) ___all politicians are crooks._____

# Standard Form

<u>Directions</u>: reconstruct the arguments in standard form (use the third-person point of view).

## 1. Non Sequitur

**Jared loves to eat; he will make a great chef!**

Since (premise) _____,

Therefore (conclusion) _____.

## 2. Either / Or

**Either give me your lunch money or plan on getting beat up after school!**

Since (premise) only two options exist, either _____

or _____,

and (implied premise) _____

Therefore (conclusion) _____.

## 3. Hasty Generalization

**Libraries ain't no fun. The Ludville library is so boring.**

Since (premise) _____,

Therefore (conclusion) _____.

# Standard Form

Directions: reconstruct the arguments in standard form.

## 4. Post Hoc

**After you walked into the room, I had an allergic reaction. I'm allergic to you.**

Since (premise) _____,

and _____

Therefore (conclusion) _____.


## 5. Abusive Ad Hominem

**My granddaughter Big Willa couldn't even keep a job at Bad Burger, so her thoughts on quantum physics and string theory have little value.**

Since (premise) _____,

Therefore (conclusion) _____.


## 6. False Analogy

**Going to school is just like going to prison. People are always telling you what to do.**

Since (premise) _____,

and _____

Therefore (conclusion) _____.

# PART 3
# ANALYZING FALLACIES

**Sample Exercise**

**Wolfgang says, "Jared loves to eat; he will make a great chef!"**

*STEP 1: reconstruct the argument in standard form.*

Since (premise) ___Jared loves to eat,___

Therefore (conclusion) ___he will make a great chef.___

*STEP 2: identify the fallacy through a process of elimination.*

Does the speaker make a personal attack?        YES (NO)

Does the speaker use the word "either" or the word "or"?        YES (NO)

Does the speaker make a generalization based on an insufficient sample?        YES (NO)

Does the conclusion follow logically from the premise?        YES (NO)

1. Therefore, what fallacy does Wolfgang commit: either/or, ad hominem, or non sequitur?

___Wolfgang___ commits ___a non sequitur___ fallacy.

2. Does it require any skill or knowledge to be a lover of food?

___It does not require any skill or knowledge to be a lover of food.___

3. Does becoming a great chef require culinary skill and cooking experience?

___Becoming a great chef requires culinary skill and cooking experience.___

*STEP 3: fill in the blanks to complete the paragraph.*

Claim: ___Wolfgang___ commits a ___non sequitur___ fallacy. He says,

Quotation: "Jared loves to eat; he will make a great chef."

Commentary:

___Wolfgang's___ conclusion that ___Jared will make a great chef___ does not follow

logically from the evidence, that ___he loves to eat.___ It does not ___require___ any skill or

___knowledge___ to be a lover of food. However, becoming a great chef requires

___culinary skill and cooking experience.___

**Sample Paragraph**

*STEP 4*: write a creative title. _____ The Hungry Chef

*STEP 5*: write out the claim, quotation, and analysis from the preceding page in paragraph form. (Double-space your work.)

The Hungry Chef

Wolfgang commits a non sequitur fallacy. He says, "Jared loves to eat; he will make a great chef." Wolfgang's conclusion that Jared will make a great chef does not follow logically from the evidence, that he loves to eat. It does not require any skill or knowledge to be a lover of food. However, becoming a great chef requires culinary skill and cooking experience.

**Exercise 1**

**Wolfgang says, "Jared loves to eat; he will make a great chef!"**

*STEP 1*: *reconstruct the argument in standard form.*

Since (premise) _____,

Therefore (conclusion) _____.

*STEP 2*: *identify the fallacy through a process of elimination.*

| | |
|---|---|
| Does the speaker make a personal attack? | **YES / NO** |
| Does the speaker use the word "either" or the word "or"? | **YES / NO** |
| Does the speaker assume that one event caused another event? | **YES / NO** |
| Does the conclusion follow logically from the premise? | **YES / NO** |

1. Therefore, what fallacy does Wolfgang commit: either/or, ad hominem, or non sequitur?

_____ **commits a / an** _____ **fallacy.**

2. Does it require any skill or knowledge to be a lover of food?

_____

_____

3. Does becoming a great chef require culinary skill and cooking experience?

_____

_____

*STEP 3*: *fill in the blanks to complete the paragraph.*

**Claim**: _____ commits a _____ fallacy. He says,

**Quotation**: "Jared loves to eat; he will make a great chef."

**Commentary**:

_____'s conclusion that _____

_____ does not follow logically from the evidence, that

_____. It does not _____ any

skill or _____ to be a lover of food. However, becoming a great

chef requires _____

_____

22

*STEP 4*: write a creative title. _____

*STEP 5*: write out the claim, quotation, and analysis from the preceding page in paragraph form.
    (Double-space your work.)

_____

_____

_____

_____

_____

_____

_____

_____

_____

_____

_____

_____

_____

_____

_____

_____

_____

_____

_____

_____

_____

_____

_____

_____

**Exercise 2**

**Dewey said, "Libraries ain't no fun. The Ludville library is so boring."**

*STEP 1*: *reconstruct the argument in standard form.*

Since (premise) _____,

Therefore (conclusion) _____.

*STEP 2*: *identify the fallacy through a process of elimination.*

| | |
|---|---|
| Does the speaker make a personal attack? | **YES / NO** |
| Does the speaker use the word "either" or the word "or"? | **YES / NO** |
| Does the speaker make a generalization based on an insufficient sample? | **YES / NO** |

1. What fallacy does Dewey commit: ad hominem, either/or, or hasty generalization?

_____

_____

2. Dewey bases his conclusion on what evidence?

_____

_____

3. Is the Ludville library representative of all libraries?

_____

_____

*STEP 3*: *fill in the blanks to complete the paragraph.*

**Claim**: _____ makes _____:

**Quotation**: "Libraries ain't no fun. The Ludville library is so boring."

**Commentary**:

_____ generalizes that _____ _____ are boring

based on insufficient evidence, that the _____ _____ is

boring; however, the Ludville library is just _____ library and does not represent

_____ libraries.

**STEP 4**: *write a creative title.* _____

**STEP 5**: *write out the claim, quotation, and analysis from the preceding page in paragraph form.*
       (Double-space your work.)

_____

_____

_____

_____

_____

_____

_____

_____

_____

_____

_____

_____

_____

_____

_____

_____

_____

_____

_____

_____

_____

_____

**Exercise 3**

**"Being homeless is like being on an extended camping trip. You get to sleep under the stars and experience the joy of roughing it!" --Senator Von Onionstien**

*STEP 1: reconstruct the argument in standard form.*

Since (premise) _____

_____,

Therefore (conclusion) _____.

*STEP 2: identify the fallacy through a process of elimination.*

Does the speaker make a personal attack?                              **YES / NO**

Does the speaker assume that one event caused another event?         **YES / NO**

Does the speaker make a false comparison?                            **YES / NO**

1. What fallacy does Von Onionstien commit: ad hominem, post hoc, or false analogy?

_____

_____

2. Do most people camp because they enjoy it?

_____

3. Are most homeless people living on the street for pleasure?

_____

_____

*STEP 3: fill in the blanks to complete the paragraph.*

**Claim**: _____ commits a

_____ _____ fallacy. He says,

**Quotation**: "Being homeless is like being on an extended camping trip. You get to sleep under the stars and experience the joy of roughing it!"

**Commentary**:

_____ assumes that because going camping and being

_____ are alike in one way, in that they both involve sleeping

_____, that they are alike in other ways. They differ in that most

people _____ because they _____ it. However, most homeless

_____ are not living on the _____ for _____.

**STEP 4**: *write a creative title.* _____

**STEP 5**: *write out the claim, quotation, and analysis from the preceding page in paragraph form.*
    (Double-space your work.)

_____

_____

_____

_____

_____

_____

_____

_____

_____

_____

_____

_____

_____

_____

_____

_____

_____

_____

_____

_____

_____

## Exercise 4

**Niki told Artemus, "Girlfriend, either do what your man says or plan on never having a boyfriend!"**

*STEP 1*: *reconstruct the argument in standard form.*

Since (premise) _____

_____,

and (implied premise) _____

Therefore (conclusion) _____.

*STEP 2*: *identify the fallacy through a process of elimination.*

| | |
|---|---|
| Does the speaker make a personal attack? | **YES / NO** |
| Does the speaker assume that one event caused another event? | **YES / NO** |
| Does the speaker make a false comparison? | **YES / NO** |
| Does the speaker use the word "either" or the word "or"? | **YES / NO** |

1. What fallacy does Niki commit: ad hominem, post hoc, false analogy, or either/or?

_____

2. Do all boyfriends require obedience from their girlfriends?

_____

_____

3. What other traits besides subservience do people look for in mates?

_____

_____

_____

*STEP 3*: *fill in the blanks to complete the paragraph.*

**Claim**: _____ commits a / an _____ fallacy. She says,

**Quotation**: "Girlfriend, either do what your man says, or plan on never having a boyfriend!"

**Commentary**:

Niki suggests that only two options exist: either _____

or _____

However, there are other options: _____

_____

***STEP 4****: write a creative title.* _____

***STEP 5****: write out the claim, quotation, and analysis from the preceding page in paragraph form.*

_____

_____

_____

_____

_____

_____

_____

_____

_____

_____

_____

_____

_____

_____

_____

_____

_____

_____

_____

_____

_____

_____

_____

_____

## Exercise 5

**Mr. Keen said, "This Arctic musk oil really works to attract the opposite sex. I put some on yesterday, and Mindy came over and smiled at me."**

*STEP 1*: *reconstruct the argument in standard form.*

Since (premise) _____

_____,

Therefore (conclusion) _____.

*STEP 2*: *identify the fallacy through a process of elimination.*

| | |
|---|---|
| Does the speaker make a personal attack? | **YES / NO** |
| Does the speaker assume that one event caused another event? | **YES / NO** |
| Does the speaker make a false comparison? | **YES / NO** |
| Does the speaker use the word "either" or the word "or"? | **YES / NO** |

1. What fallacy does Keen commit: ad hominem, post hoc, false analogy or either/or?

   _____

2. Does a smile always indicate attraction?

   _____

3. Could someone smile just to be nice?

   _____

*STEP 3*: *fill in the blanks to complete the paragraph.*

**Claim**: _____ commits a /an _____ fallacy:

**Quotation**: "This Arctic musk oil really works to attract the opposite sex. I put some on yesterday, and Mindy came over and smiled at me."

**Commentary**:

Mr. Keen assumes that because event A, applying the _____

preceded event B, _____, that the first

event caused the second. A smile does not always indicate _____.

Mindy could be smiling at Mr. Keen because _____.

30

***STEP 4****: write a creative title.* _____

***STEP 5****: write out the claim, quotation, and analysis from the preceding page in paragraph form.*

_____

_____

_____

_____

_____

_____

_____

_____

_____

_____

_____

_____

_____

_____

_____

_____

_____

_____

_____

_____

_____

_____

_____

_____

_____

## Exercise 6

**Phenomena said, "When Epiphany eats salad, she gets salad dressing all over her big mouth, so any advice she has about manners in school is not worth listening to."**

*STEP 1*: reconstruct the argument in standard form.

Since (premise) _____ ,

Therefore (conclusion) _____ .

_____

*STEP 2*: identify the fallacy through a process of elimination.

| | |
|---|---|
| Does the speaker assume that one event caused another event? | **YES / NO** |
| Does the speaker make a false comparison? | **YES / NO** |
| Does the speaker use the word "either" or the word "or"? | **YES / NO** |
| Does the speaker make a generalization based on an insufficient sample? | **YES / NO** |
| Does the speaker make a personal attack? | **YES / NO** |

1. What fallacy does Phenomena commit: ad hominem, either/or, non sequitur, hasty generalization, post hoc, or false analogy?

_____

_____

*STEP 3*: fill in the blanks to complete the paragraph.

**Claim**: _____ commits a / an _____

_____ fallacy. She says,

**Quotation**: "When Epiphany eats she gets salad dressing all over big her mouth, so any advice she has about manners in school is not worth listening to."

**Commentary**:

_____ attacks _____ instead of focusing

on the issue of _____ .

The fact that Epiphany has poor eating habits it does not mean that _____

_____

_____

32

***STEP 4***: *write a creative title.* _____

***STEP 5***: *write out the claim, quotation, and analysis from the preceding page in paragraph form.*

_____

_____

_____

_____

_____

_____

_____

_____

_____

_____

_____

_____

_____

_____

_____

_____

_____

_____

_____

_____

_____

_____

_____

_____

**Exercise 7**

**Arnold complained: "Weight lifting is the same as mowing the lawn; you get all sweaty and tired, and then the following week you have to do it all over again!"**

*STEP 1*: *reconstruct the argument in standard form.*

Since (premise) _____,

Therefore (conclusion) _____.

*STEP 2*: *identify the fallacy through a process of elimination.*

Does the speaker assume that one event caused another event?   **YES / NO**

Does the speaker make a false comparison?   **YES / NO**

Does the speaker use the word "either" or the word "or"?   **YES / NO**

Does the speaker make a personal attack?   **YES / NO**

1. What fallacy does Arnold commit: ad hominem, either/or, non sequitur, hasty generalization, post hoc, or false analogy?

   _____

2. Do weight lifting and yard work require physical effort that must be expended regularly?

   _____

   _____

3. Is yard work as effective as weight lifting for building muscle and strength?

   _____

   _____

*STEP 3*: *fill in the blanks to complete the paragraph.*

**Claim**: _____ commits a / an _____

fallacy. He says,

**Quotation**: "Weight lifting is like mowing the lawn; you get all sweaty and tired, and then the

following week you have to do it all over again!"

**Commentary**:

_____ assumes that because _____ and

_____ are alike in one way, in that they require

_____ and must be expended regularly, that they are

alike in other ways. The two things differ in that _____

is not as effective as weight lifting for building _____.

34

***STEP 4***: *write a creative title.* _____

***STEP 5***: *write out the claim, quotation, and analysis from the preceding page in paragraph form.*

_____

_____

_____

_____

_____

_____

_____

_____

_____

_____

_____

_____

_____

_____

_____

_____

_____

_____

_____

_____

_____

_____

_____

_____

_____

# Exercise 8

**Serendipity said, "I need to do better in school, so I should go shopping for shoes."**

*STEP 1*: reconstruct the argument in standard form.

Since (premise) _____,

Therefore (conclusion) _____.

*STEP 2*: identify the fallacy through a process of elimination.

| | |
|---|---|
| Does the speaker make a personal attack? | **YES / NO** |
| Does the speaker assume that one event caused another event? | **YES / NO** |
| Does the speaker make a false comparison? | **YES / NO** |
| Does the speaker use the word "either" or the word "or"? | **YES / NO** |
| Does the speaker make a generalization based on an insufficient sample? | **YES / NO** |
| Does the conclusion follow logically from the premise? | **YES / NO** |

1. What fallacy does Serendipity commit: ad hominem, post hoc, false analogy, either/or, hasty generalization, or non sequitur?

_____

_____

*STEP 3*: fill in the blanks to complete the paragraph.

**Claim**: Serendipity commits a / an _____ fallacy. She says,

**Quotation**: "I need to do better in school, so I should go shopping for shoes."

**Commentary**:

_____'s conclusion that _____

_____ does not follow logically from the preceding

statement, that _____.

To improve _____ one must study hard. Shopping will

do nothing to _____ Serendipity's GPA.

***STEP 4***: *write a creative title.* _____

***STEP 5***: *write out the claim, quotation, and analysis from the preceding page in paragraph form.*

_____

_____

_____

_____

_____

_____

_____

_____

_____

_____

_____

_____

_____

_____

_____

_____

_____

_____

_____

_____

_____

_____

_____

_____

_____

# Exercise 9

**Juan Carlos said, "Gypsy curses are real! My 98-year-old Grandma had one put on her, and the next year she choked on a triple-decker Bad Burger and died."**

*STEP 1*: *reconstruct the argument in standard form.*

Since (premise) _____

_____,

Therefore (conclusion) _____.

*STEP 2*: *identify the fallacy through a process of elimination.*

| | |
|---|---|
| Does the speaker make a personal attack? | **YES / NO** |
| Does the speaker assume that one event caused another event? | **YES / NO** |
| Does the speaker make a false comparison? | **YES / NO** |
| Does the speaker use the word "either" or the word "or"? | **YES / NO** |
| Does the speaker make a generalization based on an insufficient sample? | **YES / NO** |
| Does the conclusion follow logically from the premise? | **YES / NO** |

1. What fallacy does Juan Carlos commit: ad hominem, post hoc, false analogy, either/or, hasty generalization, or non sequitur?

_____

*STEP 3*: *fill in the blanks to complete the paragraph.*

**Claim**: _____ commits a / an _____

fallacy. He says,

**Quotation**: "Gypsy curses are real! My 98-year-old Grandma had one put on her, and the next year she choked on a triple-decker Bad Burger and died."

**Commentary**:

_____ assumes that because event A, _____

_____,

preceded event B, _____, that the

first event caused the second. His grandma could have died of _____

_____. After all she was _____ years old.

***STEP 4***: *write a creative title.* _____

***STEP 5***: *write out the claim, quotation, and analysis from the preceding page in paragraph form.*

_____
_____
_____
_____
_____
_____
_____
_____
_____
_____
_____
_____
_____
_____
_____
_____
_____
_____
_____
_____
_____
_____
_____

## Exercise 10

**Hans said, "Listen, you nincompoop, either use my secret break dancing methods or plan on getting served at the senior's division of the world championships in Iceland this fall!"**

*STEP 1*: *reconstruct the argument in standard form.*

Since (premise) _____

_____ ,

and (implied premise) _____

Therefore (conclusion) _____ .

*STEP 2*: *identify the fallacy through a process of elimination.*

| | |
|---|---|
| Does the speaker make a personal attack? | **YES / NO** |
| Does the speaker assume that one event caused another event? | **YES / NO** |
| Does the speaker make a false comparison? | **YES / NO** |
| Does the speaker use the word "either" or the word "or"? | **YES / NO** |
| Does the speaker make a generalization based on an insufficient sample? | **YES / NO** |

1. What fallacy does Hans commit: ad hominem, post hoc, false analogy, either/or, hasty generalization, or non sequitur?

_____

*STEP 3*: *fill in the blanks to complete the paragraph.*

**Claim**: _____ commits a / an _____ fallacy. He says,

**Quotation**: "Listen, you nincompoop, either use my secret break dancing methods or plan on getting served at the senior's division of the world championships in Iceland this fall!"

**Commentary**:

_____ gives only two options: either _____

_____ or _____ .

However, other options exist. For example, _____

_____

_____

***STEP 4****: write a creative title.* _____

***STEP 5****: write out the claim, quotation, and analysis from the preceding page in paragraph form.*

_____

_____

_____

_____

_____

_____

_____

_____

_____

_____

_____

_____

_____

_____

_____

_____

_____

_____

_____

_____

_____

_____

_____

_____

_____

# Exercise 11

**Fallacy Boy said, "How can that chicken hawk President Curly Von Onionstien reinstate the draft when he was too scared to even serve in the armed forces?"**

*STEP 1*: *reconstruct the argument in standard form.*

Since (premise) _____,

Therefore (conclusion) _____.

*STEP 2*: *identify the fallacy through a process of elimination.*

| | |
|---|---|
| Does the speaker make a personal attack? | **YES / NO** |
| Does the speaker assume that one event caused another event? | **YES / NO** |
| Does the speaker make a false comparison? | **YES / NO** |
| Does the speaker use the word "either" or the word "or"? | **YES / NO** |
| Does the speaker make a generalization based on an insufficient sample? | **YES / NO** |
| Does the conclusion follow logically from the premise? | **YES / NO** |

1. What fallacy does Fallacy Boy commit: ad hominem, post hoc, false analogy, either/or, hasty generalization, or non sequitur?

_____

_____

*STEP 3*: *fill in the blanks to complete the paragraph.*

**Claim**: _____ commits a / an _____ fallacy. He says,

**Quotation**: "How can that chicken hawk President Curly Von Onionstien reinstate the draft when he was too scared to even serve in the armed forces?"

**Commentary**:

_____ attacks _____

instead of focusing on the issue, _____.

Just because _____

_____ it does not mean that _____

_____

42

**STEP 4**: *write a creative title.* _____

**STEP 5**: *write out the claim, quotation, and analysis from the preceding page in paragraph form.*

_____

_____

_____

_____

_____

_____

_____

_____

_____

_____

_____

_____

_____

_____

_____

_____

_____

_____

_____

_____

_____

_____

_____

## Exercise 12

**Skater Boy told his skeptical parents, "Skating is a good career. Tony Hawk makes millions!"**

*STEP 1*: *reconstruct the argument in standard form.*

Since (premise) _____,

Therefore (conclusion) _____.

*STEP 2*: *identify the fallacy through a process of elimination.*

| | |
|---|---|
| Does the speaker make a personal attack? | **YES / NO** |
| Does the speaker assume that one event caused another event? | **YES / NO** |
| Does the speaker make a false comparison? | **YES / NO** |
| Does the speaker use the word "either" or the word "or"? | **YES / NO** |
| Does the speaker make a generalization based on an insufficient sample? | **YES / NO** |

1. What fallacy does Skater Boy commit: ad hominem, post hoc, false analogy, either/or, hasty generalization, or non sequitur?

_____

*STEP 3*: *fill in the blanks to complete the paragraph.*

**Claim**: _____ makes a / an _____

_____. He says,

**Quotation**: "Skating is a good career. Tony Hawk makes millions!"

**Commentary**:

_____ generalizes that _____

_____ based on insufficient evidence: that _____

_____

Tony _____ is the world's most successful _____

and does not represent the success of all professional _____ boarders.

44

***STEP 4****: write a creative title.* _____

***STEP 5****: write out the claim, quotation, and analysis from the preceding page in paragraph form.*

_____

_____

_____

_____

_____

_____

_____

_____

_____

_____

_____

_____

_____

_____

_____

_____

_____

_____

_____

_____

_____

_____

_____

_____

_____

## Exercise 13

**Tika shouted, "If the colonists could rebel against England during the American Revolution, then I should be able to rebel against my controlling parents!"**

*STEP 1*: *reconstruct the argument in standard form.*

Since (premise) _____ ,

Therefore (conclusion) _____ .

*STEP 2*: *identify the fallacy through a process of elimination.*

| | |
|---|---|
| Does the speaker make a personal attack? | **YES / NO** |
| Does the speaker assume that one event caused another event? | **YES / NO** |
| Does the speaker make a false comparison? | **YES / NO** |
| Does the speaker use the word "either" or the word "or"? | **YES / NO** |
| Does the speaker make a generalization based on an insufficient sample? | **YES / NO** |

1. What fallacy does Tika commit: ad hominem, post hoc, false analogy, either/or, hasty generalization, or non sequitur?

_____

*STEP 3*: *fill in the blanks to complete the paragraph.*

**Claim**: _____ commits a / an _____ fallacy. She says,

**Quotation**: "If the colonists could rebel against England during the American Revolution, then I should be able to rebel against my controlling parents!"

**Commentary**:

Just because _____

and _____

are alike in some ways in that they both involve _____ , it does not mean they are

alike in others. They are different because England wanted to exploit the _____

while parents usually set limits on _____ to protect them.

***STEP 4****: write a creative title.* _____

***STEP 5****: write out the claim, quotation, and analysis from the preceding page in paragraph form.*

_____

_____

_____

_____

_____

_____

_____

_____

_____

_____

_____

_____

_____

_____

_____

_____

_____

_____

_____

_____

_____

_____

_____

_____

## Exercise 14

**Kriss the carb-loving kleptomaniac argues, "I have to steal doughnuts or I will starve!"**

*STEP 1*: *reconstruct the argument in standard form.*

Since (premise) _____,

and (implied premise) _____

Therefore (conclusion) _____.

*STEP 2*: *identify the fallacy through a process of elimination.*

| | |
|---|---|
| Does the speaker make a personal attack? | **YES / NO** |
| Does the speaker assume that one event caused another event? | **YES / NO** |
| Does the speaker make a false comparison? | **YES / NO** |
| Does the speaker use the word "either" or the word "or"? | **YES / NO** |
| Does the speaker make a generalization based on an insufficient sample? | **YES / NO** |

1. What fallacy does Kriss commit: ad hominem, post hoc, false analogy, either/or, or hasty generalization?

_____

*STEP 3*: *fill in the blanks to complete the paragraph.*

**Claim**: _____ commits a / an _____ fallacy. She says,

**Quotation**: "I have to steal doughnuts or I will starve!"

**Commentary**:

Kris gives only two options: either _____

or _____. However, other options exist. For example, _____

_____

_____

***STEP 4****: write a creative title.* _____

***STEP 5****: write out the claim, quotation, and analysis from the preceding page in paragraph form.*

_____

_____

_____

_____

_____

_____

_____

_____

_____

_____

_____

_____

_____

_____

_____

_____

_____

_____

_____

_____

_____

_____

_____

## Exercise 15

**Philistine said, "You gotta be kidding me. Little Big E likes flowers, poetry, and kittens! How can you even consider him for the leader of our gang, the Ludville Maggots? I thought we was tough!"**

*STEP 1*: reconstruct the argument in standard form.

Since (premise) _____ ,

Therefore (conclusion) _____ .

*STEP 2*: identify the fallacy through a process of elimination.

| | |
|---|---|
| Does the speaker make a personal attack? | **YES / NO** |
| Does the speaker assume that one event caused another event? | **YES / NO** |
| Does the speaker make a false comparison? | **YES / NO** |
| Does the speaker use the word "either" or the word "or"? | **YES / NO** |
| Does the speaker make a generalization based on an insufficient sample? | **YES / NO** |
| Does the conclusion follow logically from the premise? | **YES / NO** |

1. What fallacy does Philistine commit: ad hominem, post hoc, false analogy, either/or, hasty generalization, or non sequitur?

_____

_____

*STEP 3*: fill in the blanks to complete the paragraph.

**Claim**: _____ commits a / an _____

_____ fallacy. He says,

**Quotation**: "You gotta be kidding me. Little Big E likes flowers, poetry, and kittens! How can you even consider him for the leader of our gang, the Ludville Maggots? I thought we was tough."

**Commentary**:

_____ attacks _____

instead of addressing the issue _____ .

Just because Little Big E has a _____ side, it does not mean that

_____

He could be brutal and _____ .

***STEP 4****: write a creative title.* _____

***STEP 5****: write out the claim, quotation, and analysis from the preceding page in paragraph form.*

_____

_____

_____

_____

_____

_____

_____

_____

_____

_____

_____

_____

_____

_____

_____

_____

_____

_____

_____

_____

_____

_____

## Exercise 16

**Captain King said, "Friend, this heifer has your name on it. You need to buy it now, or you won't have any milk for your Super Corn Syrup Surprise Cereal tomorrow!"**

*STEP 1*: *reconstruct the argument in standard form.*

Since (premise) _____ ,

and (implied premise) _____

Therefore (conclusion) _____ .

*STEP 2*: *identify the fallacy through a process of elimination.*

| | |
|---|---|
| Does the speaker make a personal attack? | **YES / NO** |
| Does the speaker assume that one event caused another event? | **YES / NO** |
| Does the speaker make a false comparison? | **YES / NO** |
| Does the speaker use the word "either" or the word "or"? | **YES / NO** |
| Does the speaker make a generalization based on an insufficient sample? | **YES / NO** |
| Does the conclusion follow logically from the premise? | **YES / NO** |

1. What fallacy does King commit: ad hominem, post hoc, false analogy, either/or, hasty generalization, or non sequitur?

_____

*STEP 3*: *fill in the blanks to complete the paragraph.*

**Claim**: _____ commits a / an _____

fallacy. He says,

**Quotation**: "Friend, this heifer has your name on it. You need to buy it now, or you won't have any milk for your Super Corn Syrup Surprise Cereal tomorrow!"

**Commentary**:

_____ gives only two options: either _____

_____ or _____

However, other options exist. For example, _____

_____

_____

**STEP 4**: *write a creative title.* _____

**STEP 5**: *write out the claim, quotation, and analysis from the preceding page in paragraph form.*

_____

_____

_____

_____

_____

_____

_____

_____

_____

_____

_____

_____

_____

_____

_____

_____

_____

_____

_____

_____

**Exercise 17**

**Hamlet said, "Pork tastes terrible; pickled hog hooves taste gross!"**

*STEP 1*: *reconstruct the argument in standard form.*

Since (premise) _____,

Therefore (conclusion) _____.

*STEP 2*: *identify the fallacy through a process of elimination.*

| | |
|---|---|
| Does the speaker make a personal attack? | **YES / NO** |
| Does the speaker assume that one event caused another event? | **YES / NO** |
| Does the speaker make a false comparison? | **YES / NO** |
| Does the speaker use the word "either" or the word "or"? | **YES / NO** |
| Does the speaker make a generalization based on an insufficient sample? | **YES / NO** |

1. What fallacy does Hamlet commit: ad hominem, post hoc, false analogy, either/or, hasty generalization, or non sequitur?

_____

_____

*STEP 3*: *fill in the blanks to complete the paragraph.*

**Claim**: _____ makes a _____:

**Quotation**: "Pork tastes terrible; pickled hog hooves taste gross!"

**Commentary**:

_____ generalizes that _____

_____ based on insufficient evidence, that _____

_____; however, _____

_____ are just _____ part of the pig and do not

_____ other more tasty cuts.

***STEP 4****: write a creative title.* _____

***STEP 5****: write out the claim, quotation, and analysis from the preceding page in paragraph form.*

_____
_____
_____
_____
_____
_____
_____
_____
_____
_____
_____
_____
_____
_____
_____
_____
_____
_____
_____
_____
_____
_____
_____
_____

## Exercise 18

**Adonis said to Lenore, "You're going to take your parents' advice on dating? But they're so old and ugly!"**

*STEP 1*: *reconstruct the argument in standard form.*

Since (premise) _____,

Therefore (conclusion) _____.

*STEP 2*: *identify the fallacy through a process of elimination.*

| | |
|---|---|
| Does the speaker make a personal attack? | **YES / NO** |
| Does the speaker assume that one event caused another event? | **YES / NO** |
| Does the speaker make a false comparison? | **YES / NO** |
| Does the speaker use the word "either" or the word "or"? | **YES / NO** |
| Does the speaker make a generalization based on an insufficient sample? | **YES / NO** |

1. What fallacy does Adonis commit: ad hominem, post hoc, false analogy, either/or, hasty generalization, or non sequitur?

_____

_____

*STEP 3*: *fill in the blanks to complete the paragraph.*

**Claim**: _____ commits a / an _____ fallacy. He says,

**Quotation**: "You're going to take your parents' advice on dating? But they're so old and ugly!"

**Commentary**:

_____ attacks _____ age and

physical _____ and not the issue, _____.

Just because Lenore's parents are _____ and _____

it does not mean that their advice about _____ is wrong. Adonis should

focus on the issue of _____ advice, and not _____

_____

56

**STEP 4**: *write a creative title.* _____

**STEP 5**: *write out the claim, quotation, and analysis from the preceding page in paragraph form.*

_____

_____

_____

_____

_____

_____

_____

_____

_____

_____

_____

_____

_____

_____

_____

_____

_____

_____

_____

_____

**Exercise 19**

**Stewart Pidd said, "Jo-Jo loves playing video games; he will make an excellent video game designer."**

*STEP 1*: *reconstruct the argument in standard form.*

Since (premise) _____,

Therefore (conclusion) _____.

*STEP 2*: *identify the fallacy through a process of elimination.*

| | |
|---|---|
| Does the speaker make a personal attack? | **YES / NO** |
| Does the speaker assume that one event caused another event? | **YES / NO** |
| Does the speaker make a false comparison? | **YES / NO** |
| Does the speaker use the word "either" or the word "or"? | **YES / NO** |
| Does the speaker make a generalization based on an insufficient sample? | **YES / NO** |
| Does the conclusion follow logically from the premise? | **YES / NO** |

1. What fallacy does Pidd commit: ad hominem, post hoc, false analogy, either/or, hasty generalization, or non sequitur?

_____

_____

*STEP 3*: *fill in the blanks to complete the paragraph.*

**Claim**: _____ commits a / an _____ fallacy. He says,

**Quotation**: "Jo-Jo loves playing video games; he will make an excellent video game designer."

**Commentary**:

_____'s conclusion that _____

_____does not follow logically from the preceding

statement, that _____.

Designing _____ _____ requires extensive understanding of

_____ programming along with the ability to do the hard work of

creating a good game. Loving to play video games requires _____

_____

**STEP 4**: *write a creative title.* _____

**STEP 5**: *write out the claim, quotation, and analysis from the preceding page in paragraph form.*

_____

_____

_____

_____

_____

_____

_____

_____

_____

_____

_____

_____

_____

_____

_____

_____

_____

_____

_____

_____

_____

_____

_____

_____

# PART 4
# USING TEMPLATES

**Sample Exercise**

> Jarvis shouted, "Paying taxes is like highway robbery. You hand over your hard-earned money to no-good criminals against your will."

*STEP 1*: *reconstruct the argument in standard form.*

Since (premise) _paying taxes and getting robbed involve giving up money against one's will,_

Therefore (conclusion) _paying taxes is like highway robbery._

## Templates

### Either / Or

[Insert speaker's name] constructs an either / or fallacy: "Insert quotation." [S/he] suggests that only two options exist: either [name first option], or [name second option]. In fact there are more: [give, in detail, other options].

### Post Hoc

[Insert speaker's name] commits a post hoc fallacy: "Insert quotation." [S/he] assumes that because event A, [name event], came before event B, [name event], that therefore, event A caused event B. [Insert name] fails to show a causal relationship between [insert event A] and [insert event B], so [s/he] should not assume that the first event caused the second. [Provide detailed examples of other plausible causes].

### Abusive Ad Hominem

[Insert speaker's name] offers an ineffective rebuttal by employing an ad hominem fallacy. [S/he] states, "Insert quotation." [Insert speaker's name] attacks [name the person being attacked] by [explain the form of the attack] instead of focusing on the issue, [name the issue]. The fact that [name the person being attacked] [point out negative trait] does not invalidate [his / her] argument.

### False Analogy

[Insert speaker's name] creates a false analogy. [S/he] says, "Insert quotation." Just because [first variable] and [second variable] are alike in some ways, in that they [explain how they are alike], it does not mean that they are alike in others. [Give specific examples of how they are different].

**Sample Paragraph**

**Template Tip**

When plugging your variables into the false analogy template, make sure you have parallel structure. The noun "Robbery" and participle phrase "paying taxes" are not parallel. "Getting robbed" and "paying taxes" are parallel in structure. "Robbery" and "taxes" are also parallel.

*STEP 2*: write a creative title. ___Robbery is Taxing___

*STEP 3*: choose the correct template from the previous page and write a paragraph.

Jarvis creates a false analogy. He says, "Paying taxes is like highway robbery. You hand over your hard-earned money to no-good criminals against your will." Just because robbery and taxes are alike in some ways, in that they both involve handing over hard earned money, usually against one's will, it does not mean that they are alike in others. Taxes go toward government services. Robbers spend the money on themselves.

> **False Analogy Template**

# Exercise 20

**Jarvis shouted, "Paying taxes is like highway robbery. You hand over your hard-earned money to no-good criminals against your will."**

*STEP 1*: *reconstruct the argument in standard form.*

Since (premise) _____,

_____,

Therefore (conclusion) _____.

## Templates

### Either / Or

[Insert speaker's name] constructs an either / or fallacy: "Insert quotation." [S/he] suggests that only two options exist: either [name first option], or [name second option]. In fact there are more: [give, in detail, other options].

### Post Hoc

[Insert speaker's name] commits a post hoc fallacy: "Insert quotation." [S/he] assumes that because event A, [name event], came before event B, [name event], that therefore, event A caused event B. [Insert name] fails to show a causal relationship between [insert event A] and [insert event B], so [s/he] should not assume that the first event caused the second. [Provide detailed examples of other plausible causes].

### Abusive Ad Hominem

[Insert speaker's name] offers an ineffective rebuttal by employing an ad hominem fallacy. [S/he] states, "Insert quotation." [Insert speaker's name] attacks [name the person being attacked] by [explain the form of the attack] instead of focusing on the issue, [name the issue]. The fact that [name the person being attacked] [point out the negative trait] does not invalidate [his / her] argument.

### False Analogy

[Insert speaker's name] creates a false analogy. [S/he] says, "Insert quotation." Just because [first variable] and [second variable] are alike in some ways, in that they [explain how they are alike], it does not mean that they are alike in others. [Give specific examples of how they are different].

## Template Tip

Use parallel structure with the false analogy template. The noun "Robbery" and participle phrase "paying taxes" are not parallel. "Getting robbed" and "paying taxes" are parallel in structure. "Robbery" and "taxes" are also parallel.

*STEP 2*: write a creative title._____

*STEP 3*: choose the correct template from the previous page and write a paragraph.

_____

_____

_____

_____

_____

_____

_____

_____

_____

_____

_____

_____

_____

_____

_____

_____

_____

_____

_____

_____

# Exercise 21

**Ahab told Ishmael, "Whales are not dangerous. I swam with some at Whaleworld last winter, and it was wonderful!"**

*STEP 1*: *reconstruct the argument in standard form.*

Since (premise) _____,

Therefore (conclusion) _____.

## Templates

### Non Sequitur

[Insert speaker's name] uses the non sequitur fallacy. [S/he] says, "Insert quotation." The conclusion that [insert conclusion] does not follow logically from the idea that supposedly supports it, that [insert faulty supporting idea]. [Explain in detail why the conclusion does not follow logically from the evidence].

### Either / Or

[Insert speaker's name] commits an either / or fallacy: "Insert quotation." [S/he] suggests that only two options exist: either [name first option], or [name second option]. In fact there are more: [give other options].

### Post Hoc

[Insert speaker's name] commits a post hoc fallacy: "Insert quotation." [S/he] assumes that because event A, [name event], came before event B, [name event], that therefore, event A caused event B. [Insert name] fails to show a causal relationship between [insert event A] and [insert event B], so [s/he] should not assume that the first event caused the second. [Provide detailed examples of other plausible causes].

### Hasty Generalization

[Insert speaker's name] makes a hasty generalization: "Insert quotation." [Insert speaker's name] generalizes that [insert the generalization/conclusion] based on insufficient evidence, that [identify evidence/premise]; however, [explain why the particular "sample" does represent to the entire "population"].

### Abusive Ad Hominem

[Insert speaker's name] offers an ineffective rebuttal by employing an ad hominem fallacy. [S/he] states, "Insert quotation." [Insert speaker's name] attacks [name the person being attacked] by [explain the form of the attack] instead of focusing on the issue, [name the issue]. The fact that [name the person being attacked] [point out negative trait] does not invalidate [his / her] argument.

## Template Tip

When using the hasty generalization template, talk about the size of the sample that supposedly supports the generalization. Explain why it is too small. Be specific.

*STEP 2*: write a creative title._____

*STEP 3*: choose the correct template from the previous page and write a paragraph.

_____

_____

_____

_____

_____

_____

_____

**Exercise 22**

### Rama said, "Yip-yip is a darn good skater; therefore, he must be a poor student."

*STEP 1*: *reconstruct the argument in standard form.*

Since (premise) _____,

Therefore (conclusion) _____.

## Templates

**False Analogy**

[Insert speaker's name] creates a false analogy. [S/he] says, "Insert quotation." Just because [first variable] and [second variable] are alike in some ways, in that they [explain how they are alike], it does not mean that they are alike in others. [Explain in detail how they are different].

**Either / Or**

[Insert speaker's name] commits an either / or fallacy: "Insert quotation." [S/he] suggests that only two options exist: either [name first option], or [name second option]. In fact there are more: [give other options].

**Non Sequitur**

[Insert speaker's name] uses the non sequitur fallacy. [S/he] says, "Insert quotation." The conclusion that [insert conclusion] does not follow logically from the idea that supposedly supports it, that [insert faulty supporting idea]. [Explain in detail why the conclusion does not follow logically from the evidence].

**Post Hoc**

[Insert speaker's name] commits a post hoc fallacy: "Insert quotation." [S/he] assumes that because event A, [name event], came before event B, [name event], that therefore, event A caused event B. [Insert name] fails to show a causal relationship between [insert event A] and [insert event B], so [s/he] should not assume that the first event caused the second. [Provide detailed examples of other plausible causes].

**Abusive Ad Hominem**

[Insert speaker's name] offers an ineffective rebuttal by employing an ad hominem fallacy. [S/he] states, "Insert quotation." [Insert speaker's name] attacks [name the person being attacked] by [explain the form of the attack] instead of focusing on the issue, [name the issue]. The fact that [name the person being attacked] [point out negative trait] does not invalidate [his / her] argument.

# Template Tip

When using the non sequitur template, talk about the specifics of the faulty premise. Avoid generalizations. Explain in detail why the premise does not support the conclusion.

*STEP 2*: write a creative title._____

*STEP 3*: choose the correct template from the previous page and write a paragraph.

_____

_____

_____

_____

_____

_____

_____

_____

_____

_____

_____

_____

_____

_____

_____

_____

_____

_____

_____

_____

_____

_____

# Exercise 23

## Benedict said, "America: either love it or freeze to death in Canada."

*STEP 1*: reconstruct the argument in standard form.

Since (premise) _____,

_____,

and (implied premise) _____

Therefore (conclusion) _____.

## Templates

### Hasty Generalization
[Insert speaker's name] makes a hasty generalization: "Insert quotation." [Insert speaker's name] generalizes that [insert the generalization/conclusion] based on insufficient evidence, that [identify evidence/premise]; however, [explain why the particular "sample" does represent to the entire "population"].

### Non Sequitur
[Insert speaker's name] uses the non sequitur fallacy. [S/he] says, "Insert quotation." The conclusion that [insert conclusion] does not follow logically from the idea that supposedly supports it, that [insert faulty supporting idea]. [Explain in detail why the conclusion does not follow logically from the evidence].

### False Analogy
[Insert speaker's name] creates a false analogy. [S/he] says, "Insert quotation." Just because [first variable] and [second variable] are alike in some ways, in that they [explain how they are alike], it does not mean that they are alike in others. [Explain in detail how they are different].

### Either / Or
[Insert speaker's name] commits an either / or fallacy: "Insert quotation." [S/he] suggests that only two options exist: either [name first option], or [name second option]. In fact there are more: [give other options].

### Post Hoc
[Insert speaker's name] commits a post hoc fallacy: "Insert quotation." [S/he] assumes that because event A, [name event], came before event B, [name event], that therefore, event A caused event B. [Insert name] fails to show a causal relationship between [insert event A] and [insert event B], so [s/he] should not assume that the first event caused the second. [Provide detailed examples of other plausible causes].

### Abusive Ad Hominem
[Insert speaker's name] offers an ineffective rebuttal by employing an ad hominem fallacy. [S/he] states, "Insert quotation." [Insert speaker's name] attacks [name the person being attacked] by [explain the form of the attack] instead of focusing on the issue, [name the issue]. The fact that [name the person being attacked] [point out negative trait] does not invalidate [his / her] argument.

**Template Tip**

When using the either/or template, stay in the third person point of view. Do not give second person commands:

`"Two options exist: love America or freeze to death in Canada."`

Third person point of view:

`Two options exist: one can love America or one can freeze to death in Canada.`

`Two options exist: loving America or freezing to death in Canada.`

*(Note the parallel structure in both examples)*

***STEP 2****: write a creative title.*_____

***STEP 3****: choose the correct template from the previous page and write a paragraph.*

_____

_____

_____

_____

_____

_____

_____

_____

_____

_____

_____

_____

_____

_____

_____

_____

_____

_____

# Exercise 24

**Ms. Interpretation complains, "Flabaurt says, 'Stop shuffling your feet!' But all that lazy bum wants to do is lie around all day and watch interior design shows on TV!"**

*STEP 1*: *reconstruct the argument in standard form.*

Since (premise) _____ ,

_____ ,

Therefore (conclusion) _____ .

## Templates

### Hasty Generalization

[Insert speaker's name] makes a hasty generalization: "Insert quotation." [Insert speaker's name] generalizes that [insert the generalization/conclusion] based on insufficient evidence, that [identify evidence/premise]; however, [explain why the particular "sample" does represent to the entire "population"].

### Non Sequitur

[Insert speaker's name] uses the non sequitur fallacy. [S/he] says, "Insert quotation." The conclusion that [insert conclusion] does not follow logically from the idea that supposedly supports it, that [insert faulty supporting idea]. [Explain in detail why the conclusion does not follow logically from the evidence].

### False Analogy

[Insert speaker's name] creates a false analogy. [S/he] says, "Insert quotation." Just because [first variable] and [second variable] are alike in some ways, in that they [explain how they are alike], it does not mean that they are alike in others. [Explain in detail how they are different].

### Either / Or

[Insert speaker's name] commits an either / or fallacy: "Insert quotation." [S/he] suggests that only two options exist: either [name first option], or [name second option]. In fact there are more: [give other options].

### Post Hoc

[Insert speaker's name] commits a post hoc fallacy: "Insert quotation." [S/he] assumes that because event A, [name event], came before event B, [name event], that therefore, event A caused event B. [Insert name] fails to show a causal relationship between [insert event A] and [insert event B], so [s/he] should not assume that the first event caused the second. [Provide detailed examples of other plausible causes].

### Abusive Ad Hominem

[Insert speaker's name] offers an ineffective rebuttal by employing an ad hominem fallacy. [S/he] states, "Insert quotation." [Insert speaker's name] attacks [name the person being attacked] by [explain the form of the attack] instead of focusing on the issue, [name the issue]. The fact that [name the person being attacked] [point out negative trait] does not invalidate [his / her] argument.

**Template Tip**

Use single quotation marks when quoting within double quotation marks.

My sister told me, "Blathering Bob says, 'I don't blather. I just like to talk a lot.'"

*STEP 2*: write a creative title._____

*STEP 3*: choose the correct template from the previous page and write a paragraph.

_____

_____

_____

_____

_____

_____

_____

_____

_____

_____

_____

_____

_____

_____

_____

_____

_____

_____

_____

_____

# Exercise 25

**Aristotle proclaimed, "I did a lot of work in Professor Plato's philosophy class, so I deserve an 'A'!"**

*STEP 1*: reconstruct the argument in standard form.

Since (premise) _____,

_____,

Therefore (conclusion) _____.

## Templates

### Hasty Generalization

[Insert speaker's name] makes a hasty generalization: "Insert quotation." [Insert speaker's name] generalizes that [insert the generalization/conclusion] based on insufficient evidence, that [identify evidence/premise]; however, [explain why the particular "sample" does represent to the entire "population"].

### Non Sequitur

[Insert speaker's name] uses the non sequitur fallacy. [S/he] says, "Insert quotation." The conclusion that [insert conclusion] does not follow logically from the idea that supposedly supports it, that [insert faulty supporting idea]. [Explain in detail why the conclusion does not follow logically from the evidence].

### False Analogy

[Insert speaker's name] creates a false analogy. [S/he] says, "Insert quotation." Just because [first variable] and [second variable] are alike in some ways, in that they [explain how they are alike], it does not mean that they are alike in others. [Explain in detail how they are different].

### Either / Or

[Insert speaker's name] commits an either / or fallacy: "Insert quotation." [S/he] suggests that only two options exist: either [name first option], or [name second option]. In fact there are more: [give other options].

### Post Hoc

[Insert speaker's name] commits a post hoc fallacy: "Insert quotation." [S/he] assumes that because event A, [name event], came before event B, [name event], that therefore, event A caused event B. [Insert name] fails to show a causal relationship between [insert event A] and [insert event B], so [s/he] should not assume that the first event caused the second. [Provide detailed examples of other plausible causes].

### Abusive Ad Hominem

[Insert speaker's name] offers an ineffective rebuttal by employing an ad hominem fallacy. [S/he] states, "Insert quotation." [Insert speaker's name] attacks [name the person being attacked] by [explain the form of the attack] instead of focusing on the issue, [name the issue]. The fact that [name the person being attacked] [point out negative trait] does not invalidate [his / her] argument.

**Template Tip**

Avoid plugging direct quotations in the **commentary** section of the template.

*Incorrect:*
        The conclusion that "I deserve an 'A'" does not follow logically from the idea that supposedly supports it, "I did a lot of work in Mr. Plato's philosophy class."

*Correct:*
        The conclusion that Aristotle deserves an 'A' in Mr. Plato's philosophy class does not follow logically from the idea that supposedly supports it, that he did a lot of work in the class.

*STEP 2*: write a creative title._____

*STEP 3*: choose the correct template from the previous page and write a paragraph.

_____
_____
_____
_____
_____
_____
_____
_____
_____
_____
_____
_____
_____
_____
_____
_____
_____
_____
_____
_____
_____
_____

**Exercise 26**

> **Cleo said, "Of course this jellybean gives me good luck. I stuck it up my nose, and then I got a Bonzer surfboard and a Shetland pony for my birthday."**

*STEP 1*: *reconstruct the argument in standard form.*

Since (premise) _____ ,

_____ ,

Therefore (conclusion) _____ .

## Templates

### Hasty Generalization

[Insert speaker's name] makes a hasty generalization: "Insert quotation." [Insert speaker's name] generalizes that [insert the generalization/conclusion] based on insufficient evidence, that [identify evidence/premise]; however, [explain why the particular "sample" does represent to the entire "population"].

### Non Sequitur

[Insert speaker's name] uses the non sequitur fallacy. [S/he] says, "Insert quotation." The conclusion that [insert conclusion] does not follow logically from the idea that supposedly supports it, that [insert faulty supporting idea]. [Explain in detail why the conclusion does not follow logically from the evidence].

### False Analogy

[Insert speaker's name] creates a false analogy. [S/he] says, "Insert quotation." Just because [first variable] and [second variable] are alike in some ways, in that they [explain how they are alike], it does not mean that they are alike in others. [Explain in detail how they are different].

### Either / Or

[Insert speaker's name] commits an either / or fallacy: "Insert quotation." [S/he] suggests that only two options exist: either [name first option], or [name second option]. In fact there are more: [give other options].

### Post Hoc

[Insert speaker's name] commits a post hoc fallacy: "Insert quotation." [S/he] assumes that because event A, [name event], came before event B, [name event], that therefore, event A caused event B. [Insert name] fails to show a causal relationship between [insert event A] and [insert event B], so [s/he] should not assume that the first event caused the second. [Provide detailed examples of other plausible causes].

### Abusive Ad Hominem

[Insert speaker's name] offers an ineffective rebuttal by employing an ad hominem fallacy. [S/he] states, "Insert quotation." [Insert speaker's name] attacks [name the person being attacked] by [explain the form of the attack] instead of focusing on the issue, [name the issue]. The fact that [name the person being attacked] [point out negative trait] does not invalidate [his / her] argument.

## Template Tip

When plugging your event A and event B variables into the post hoc fallacy template, avoid placing an independent clause (a complete sentence) between two commas. Do not write

```
Cleo assumes that because event A, she stuck a jellybean up her nose,
came before event B, she received good birthday presents, that therefore
event A caused event B.
```

Instead rephrase the modifiers as nouns or noun phrases:

```
She assumes that because event A, sticking a jellybean up her nose, came
before event B, receiving nice birthday gifts, that therefore event A
caused event B.
```

*STEP 2*: write a creative title._____

*STEP 3*: choose the correct template from the previous page and write a paragraph.

_____
_____
_____
_____
_____
_____
_____
_____
_____
_____
_____
_____
_____
_____
_____
_____
_____
_____
_____
_____

**Exercise 27**

> **Kelly said, "Surfers are slobs. My ex-girlfriend surfs, and she always used to leave her dirty dishes next to her bed, which she never made!"**

*STEP 1*: *reconstruct the argument in standard form.*

Since (premise) _____,

_____,

Therefore (conclusion) _____.

## Templates

### Hasty Generalization
[Insert speaker's name] makes a hasty generalization: "Insert quotation." [Insert speaker's name] generalizes that [insert the generalization/conclusion] based on insufficient evidence, that [identify evidence/premise]; however, [explain why the particular "sample" does represent to the entire "population"].

### Non Sequitur
[Insert speaker's name] uses the non sequitur fallacy. [S/he] says, "Insert quotation." The conclusion that [insert conclusion] does not follow logically from the idea that supposedly supports it, that [insert faulty supporting idea]. [Explain in detail why the conclusion does not follow logically from the evidence].

### False Analogy
[Insert speaker's name] creates a false analogy. [S/he] says, "Insert quotation." Just because [first variable] and [second variable] are alike in some ways, in that they [explain how they are alike], it does not mean that they are alike in others. [Explain in detail how they are different].

### Either / Or
[Insert speaker's name] commits an either / or fallacy: "Insert quotation." [S/he] suggests that only two options exist: either [name first option], or [name second option]. In fact there are more: [give other options].

### Post Hoc
[Insert speaker's name] commits a post hoc fallacy: "Insert quotation." [S/he] assumes that because event A, [name event], came before event B, [name event], that therefore, event A caused event B. [Insert name] fails to show a causal relationship between [insert event A] and [insert event B], so [s/he] should not assume that the first event caused the second. [Provide detailed examples of other plausible causes].

### Abusive Ad Hominem
[Insert speaker's name] offers an ineffective rebuttal by employing an ad hominem fallacy. [S/he] states, "Insert quotation." [Insert speaker's name] attacks [name the person being attacked] by [explain the form of the attack] instead of focusing on the issue, [name the issue]. The fact that [name the person being attacked] [point out negative trait] does not invalidate [his / her] argument.

***STEP 2****: write a creative title.* _____

***STEP 3****: choose the correct template from the previous page and write a paragraph.*

_____

_____

_____

_____

_____

_____

_____

_____

_____

_____

_____

_____

_____

_____

_____

_____

_____

_____

_____

_____

_____

_____

# Exercise 28

**Winston said: "Cigarettes ain't dangerous. My grandma Beanbarf smoked, and she lived until she was 102 years old!"**

*STEP 1*: *reconstruct the argument in standard form.*

Since (premise) _____,

_____,

Therefore (conclusion) _____.

## Templates

### Hasty Generalization

[Insert speaker's name] makes a hasty generalization: "Insert quotation." [Insert speaker's name] generalizes that [insert the generalization/conclusion] based on insufficient evidence, that [identify evidence/premise]; however, [explain why the particular "sample" does represent to the entire "population"].

### Non Sequitur

[Insert speaker's name] uses the non sequitur fallacy. [S/he] says, "Insert quotation." The conclusion that [insert conclusion] does not follow logically from the idea that supposedly supports it, that [insert faulty supporting idea]. [Explain in detail why the conclusion does not follow logically from the evidence].

### False Analogy

[Insert speaker's name] creates a false analogy. [S/he] says, "Insert quotation." Just because [first variable] and [second variable] are alike in some ways, in that they [explain how they are alike], it does not mean that they are alike in others. [Explain in detail how they are different].

### Either / Or

[Insert speaker's name] commits an either / or fallacy: "Insert quotation." [S/he] suggests that only two options exist: either [name first option], or [name second option]. In fact there are more: [give other options].

### Post Hoc

[Insert speaker's name] commits a post hoc fallacy: "Insert quotation." [S/he] assumes that because event A, [name event], came before event B, [name event], that therefore, event A caused event B. [Insert name] fails to show a causal relationship between [insert event A] and [insert event B], so [s/he] should not assume that the first event caused the second. [Provide detailed examples of other plausible causes].

### Abusive Ad Hominem

[Insert speaker's name] offers an ineffective rebuttal by employing an ad hominem fallacy. [S/he] states, "Insert quotation." [Insert speaker's name] attacks [name the person being attacked] by [explain the form of the attack] instead of focusing on the issue, [name the issue]. The fact that [name the person being attacked] [point out negative trait] does not invalidate [his / her] argument.

***STEP 2****: write a creative title.*_____

***STEP 3****: choose the correct template from the previous page and write a paragraph.*

_____

_____

_____

_____

_____

# Exercise 29

**Faulkner asked, "You're going to take Flannery's advice about working out? Don't you know that she can't even bench press a 45-pound bar?"**

*STEP 1*: *reconstruct the argument in standard form.*

Since (premise) _____ ,

_____ ,

Therefore (conclusion) _____ .

## Templates

### Hasty Generalization
[Insert speaker's name] makes a hasty generalization: "Insert quotation." [Insert speaker's name] generalizes that [insert the generalization/conclusion] based on insufficient evidence, that [identify evidence/premise]; however, [explain why the particular "sample" does represent to the entire "population"].

### Non Sequitur
[Insert speaker's name] uses the non sequitur fallacy. [S/he] says, "Insert quotation." The conclusion that [insert conclusion] does not follow logically from the idea that supposedly supports it, that [insert faulty supporting idea]. [Explain in detail why the conclusion does not follow logically from the evidence].

### False Analogy
[Insert speaker's name] creates a false analogy. [S/he] says, "Insert quotation." Just because [first variable] and [second variable] are alike in some ways, in that they [explain how they are alike], it does not mean that they are alike in others. [Explain in detail how they are different].

### Either / Or
[Insert speaker's name] commits an either / or fallacy: "Insert quotation." [S/he] suggests that only two options exist: either [name first option], or [name second option]. In fact there are more: [give other options].

### Post Hoc
[Insert speaker's name] commits a post hoc fallacy: "Insert quotation." [S/he] assumes that because event A, [name event], came before event B, [name event], that therefore, event A caused event B. [Insert name] fails to show a causal relationship between [insert event A] and [insert event B], so [s/he] should not assume that the first event caused the second. [Provide detailed examples of other plausible causes].

### Abusive Ad Hominem
[Insert speaker's name] offers an ineffective rebuttal by employing an ad hominem fallacy. [S/he] states, "Insert quotation." [Insert speaker's name] attacks [name the person being attacked] by [explain the form of the attack] instead of focusing on the issue, [name the issue]. The fact that [name the person being attacked] [point out negative trait] does not invalidate [his / her] argument.

**Template Tip**

Guidelines for number usage:

*MLA*: Two words or less, spell the word: "forty-five."
More than two words, write the number: 454.
*APA*: As a general rule, use words for zero though nine. Use numbers for 10 or greater.

***STEP 2****: write a creative title.*_____

***STEP 3****: choose the correct template from the previous page and write a paragraph.*

_____

_____

_____

_____

_____

_____

_____

_____

_____

_____

_____

_____

_____

_____

_____

_____

_____

_____

_____

# Exercise 30

## Jealousy exclaimed, "Tina got an 'A' on her math test. *Cheater!*"

*STEP 1*: *reconstruct the argument in standard form.*


Since (premise) _____ ,

_____ ,

Therefore (conclusion) _____ .

## Templates

### Hasty Generalization

[Insert speaker's name] makes a hasty generalization: "Insert quotation." [Insert speaker's name] generalizes that [insert the generalization/conclusion] based on insufficient evidence, that [identify evidence/premise]; however, [explain why the particular "sample" does represent to the entire "population"].

### Non Sequitur

[Insert speaker's name] uses the non sequitur fallacy. [S/he] says, "Insert quotation." The conclusion that [insert conclusion] does not follow logically from the idea that supposedly supports it, that [insert faulty supporting idea]. [Explain in detail why the conclusion does not follow logically from the evidence].

### False Analogy

[Insert speaker's name] creates a false analogy. [S/he] says, "Insert quotation." Just because [first variable] and [second variable] are alike in some ways, in that they [explain how they are alike], it does not mean that they are alike in others. [Explain in detail how they are different].

### Either / Or

[Insert speaker's name] commits an either / or fallacy: "Insert quotation." [S/he] suggests that only two options exist: either [name first option], or [name second option]. In fact there are more: [give other options].

### Post Hoc

[Insert speaker's name] commits a post hoc fallacy: "Insert quotation." [S/he] assumes that because event A, [name event], came before event B, [name event], that therefore, event A caused event B. [Insert name] fails to show a causal relationship between [insert event A] and [insert event B], so [s/he] should not assume that the first event caused the second. [Provide detailed examples of other plausible causes].

### Abusive Ad Hominem

[Insert speaker's name] offers an ineffective rebuttal by employing an ad hominem fallacy. [S/he] states, "Insert quotation." [Insert speaker's name] attacks [name the person being attacked] by [explain the form of the attack] instead of focusing on the issue, [name the issue]. The fact that [name the person being attacked] [point out negative trait] does not invalidate [his / her] argument.

***STEP 2***: write a creative title._____

***STEP 3***: choose the correct template from the previous page and write a paragraph.

_____

_____

_____

_____

_____

_____

_____

_____

_____

_____

_____

_____

_____

_____

_____

_____

_____

_____

_____

_____

_____

_____

# Exercise 31

**Luna said, "Last night Jon-Jon went crazy, and there was a full moon.
I reckon that full moon just makes that dern boy crazy."**

*STEP 1*: reconstruct the argument in standard form.

Since (premise) _____,

_____,

Therefore (conclusion) _____.

## Templates

### Hasty Generalization
[Insert speaker's name] makes a hasty generalization: "Insert quotation." [Insert speaker's name] generalizes that [insert the generalization/conclusion] based on insufficient evidence, that [identify evidence/premise]; however, [explain why the particular "sample" does represent to the entire "population"].

### Non Sequitur
[Insert speaker's name] uses the non sequitur fallacy. [S/he] says, "Insert quotation." The conclusion that [insert conclusion] does not follow logically from the idea that supposedly supports it, that [insert faulty supporting idea]. [Explain in detail why the conclusion does not follow logically from the evidence].

### False Analogy
[Insert speaker's name] creates a false analogy. [S/he] says, "Insert quotation." Just because [first variable] and [second variable] are alike in some ways, in that they [explain how they are alike], it does not mean that they are alike in others. [Explain in detail how they are different].

### Either / Or
[Insert speaker's name] commits an either / or fallacy: "Insert quotation." [S/he] suggests that only two options exist: either [name first option], or [name second option]. In fact there are more: [give other options].

### Post Hoc
[Insert speaker's name] commits a post hoc fallacy: "Insert quotation." [S/he] assumes that because event A, [name event], came before event B, [name event], that therefore, event A caused event B. [Insert name] fails to show a causal relationship between [insert event A] and [insert event B], so [s/he] should not assume that the first event caused the second. [Provide detailed examples of other plausible causes].

### Abusive Ad Hominem
[Insert speaker's name] offers an ineffective rebuttal by employing an ad hominem fallacy. [S/he] states, "Insert quotation." [Insert speaker's name] attacks [name the person being attacked] by [explain the form of the attack] instead of focusing on the issue, [name the issue]. The fact that [name the person being attacked] [point out negative trait] does not invalidate [his / her] argument.

***STEP 2***: *write a creative title.* _____

***STEP 3***: *choose the correct template from the previous page and write a paragraph.*

_____

_____

_____

_____

_____

_____

_____

_____

_____

_____

_____

_____

_____

_____

_____

_____

_____

_____

_____

_____

_____

_____

_____

# Exercise 32

**Mrs. Wright said, "Left-handed people are clumsy! Lefty Liplicker was klutz city!"**

*STEP 1*: *reconstruct the argument in standard form.*

Since (premise) _____,

_____,

Therefore (conclusion) _____.

## Templates

### Hasty Generalization

[Insert speaker's name] makes a hasty generalization: "Insert quotation." [Insert speaker's name] generalizes that [insert the generalization/conclusion] based on insufficient evidence, that [identify evidence/premise]; however, [explain why the particular "sample" does represent to the entire "population"].

### Non Sequitur

[Insert speaker's name] uses the non sequitur fallacy. [S/he] says, "Insert quotation." The conclusion that [insert conclusion] does not follow logically from the idea that supposedly supports it, that [insert faulty supporting idea]. [Explain in detail why the conclusion does not follow logically from the evidence].

### False Analogy

[Insert speaker's name] creates a false analogy. [S/he] says, "Insert quotation." Just because [first variable] and [second variable] are alike in some ways, in that they [explain how they are alike], it does not mean that they are alike in others. [Explain in detail how they are different].

### Either / Or

[Insert speaker's name] commits an either / or fallacy: "Insert quotation." [S/he] suggests that only two options exist: either [name first option], or [name second option]. In fact there are more: [give other options].

### Post Hoc

[Insert speaker's name] commits a post hoc fallacy: "Insert quotation." [S/he] assumes that because event A, [name event], came before event B, [name event], that therefore, event A caused event B. [Insert name] fails to show a causal relationship between [insert event A] and [insert event B], so [s/he] should not assume that the first event caused the second. [Provide detailed examples of other plausible causes].

### Abusive Ad Hominem

[Insert speaker's name] offers an ineffective rebuttal by employing an ad hominem fallacy. [S/he] states, "Insert quotation." [Insert speaker's name] attacks [name the person being attacked] by [explain the form of the attack] instead of focusing on the issue, [name the issue]. The fact that [name the person being attacked] [point out negative trait] does not invalidate [his / her] argument.

**STEP 2**: *write a creative title.*_____

**STEP 3**: *choose the correct template from the previous page and write a paragraph.*

_____

_____

_____

_____

_____

_____

_____

_____

_____

_____

_____

_____

_____

_____

_____

_____

_____

_____

_____

_____

_____

_____

_____

**Exercise 33**

**Last year at the Ludville County Fair, Sheba the Evil Broccoli Queen said, "You either eat your broccoli or you'll be deficient in your vitamin A, boy!"**

*STEP 1*: *reconstruct the argument in standard form.*

Since (premise) _____,

and (implied premise) _____

Therefore (conclusion) _____.

## Templates

### Hasty Generalization

[Insert speaker's name] makes a hasty generalization: "Insert quotation." [Insert speaker's name] generalizes that [insert the generalization/conclusion] based on insufficient evidence, that [identify evidence/premise]; however, [explain why the particular "sample" does represent to the entire "population"].

### Non Sequitur

[Insert speaker's name] uses the non sequitur fallacy. [S/he] says, "Insert quotation." The conclusion that [insert conclusion] does not follow logically from the idea that supposedly supports it, that [insert faulty supporting idea]. [Explain in detail why the conclusion does not follow logically from the evidence].

### False Analogy

[Insert speaker's name] creates a false analogy. [S/he] says, "Insert quotation." Just because [first variable] and [second variable] are alike in some ways, in that they [explain how they are alike], it does not mean that they are alike in others. [Explain in detail how they are different].

### Either / Or

[Insert speaker's name] commits an either / or fallacy: "Insert quotation." [S/he] suggests that only two options exist: either [name first option], or [name second option]. In fact there are more: [give other options].

### Post Hoc

[Insert speaker's name] commits a post hoc fallacy: "Insert quotation." [S/he] assumes that because event A, [name event], came before event B, [name event], that therefore, event A caused event B. [Insert name] fails to show a causal relationship between [insert event A] and [insert event B], so [s/he] should not assume that the first event caused the second. [Provide detailed examples of other plausible causes].

### Abusive Ad Hominem

[Insert speaker's name] offers an ineffective rebuttal by employing an ad hominem fallacy. [S/he] states, "Insert quotation." [Insert speaker's name] attacks [name the person being attacked] by [explain the form of the attack] instead of focusing on the issue, [name the issue]. The fact that [name the person being attacked] [point out negative trait] does not invalidate [his / her] argument.

**STEP 2**: *write a creative title.*_____

**STEP 3**: *choose the correct template from the previous page and write a paragraph.*

_____

_____

_____

_____

_____

_____

_____

_____

_____

_____

_____

_____

_____

_____

_____

_____

_____

_____

_____

_____

_____

# Exercise 34

**Mr. Naipaul said, "I'm convinced that yelling at my students is the key to good teaching. Before the mid-term I screamed at the 'twits, and they all got 'A's on their tests."**

*STEP 1: reconstruct the argument in standard form.*

Since (premise) _____,

_____,

Therefore (conclusion) _____.

## Templates

### Hasty Generalization

[Insert speaker's name] makes a hasty generalization: "Insert quotation." [Insert speaker's name] generalizes that [insert the generalization/conclusion] based on insufficient evidence, that [identify evidence/premise]; however, [explain why the particular "sample" does represent to the entire "population"].

### Non Sequitur

[Insert speaker's name] uses the non sequitur fallacy. [S/he] says, "Insert quotation." The conclusion that [insert conclusion] does not follow logically from the idea that supposedly supports it, that [insert faulty supporting idea]. [Explain in detail why the conclusion does not follow logically from the evidence].

### False Analogy

[Insert speaker's name] creates a false analogy. [S/he] says, "Insert quotation." Just because [first variable] and [second variable] are alike in some ways, in that they [explain how they are alike], it does not mean that they are alike in others. [Explain in detail how they are different].

### Either / Or

[Insert speaker's name] commits an either / or fallacy: "Insert quotation." [S/he] suggests that only two options exist: either [name first option], or [name second option]. In fact there are more: [give other options].

### Post Hoc

[Insert speaker's name] commits a post hoc fallacy: "Insert quotation." [S/he] assumes that because event A, [name event], came before event B, [name event], that therefore, event A caused event B. [Insert name] fails to show a causal relationship between [insert event A] and [insert event B], so [s/he] should not assume that the first event caused the second. [Provide detailed examples of other plausible causes].

### Abusive Ad Hominem

[Insert speaker's name] offers an ineffective rebuttal by employing an ad hominem fallacy. [S/he] states, "Insert quotation." [Insert speaker's name] attacks [name the person being attacked] by [explain the form of the attack] instead of focusing on the issue, [name the issue]. The fact that [name the person being attacked] [point out negative trait] does not invalidate [his / her] argument.

***STEP 2***: write a creative title._____

***STEP 3***: choose the correct template from the previous page and write a paragraph.

_____

_____

_____

_____

_____

_____

_____

_____

_____

_____

_____

_____

_____

_____

_____

_____

_____

_____

_____

_____

_____

_____

# Exercise 35

**Brainhead told his rich girlfriend, Malaria, "Either you give me a new sports car or you don't love me!"**

*STEP 1*: *reconstruct the argument in standard form.*

Since (premise) _____,

and (implied premise) _____

Therefore (conclusion) _____.

## Templates

### Hasty Generalization
[Insert speaker's name] makes a hasty generalization: "Insert quotation." [Insert speaker's name] generalizes that [insert the generalization/conclusion] based on insufficient evidence, that [identify evidence/premise]; however, [explain why the particular "sample" does represent to the entire "population"].

### Non Sequitur
[Insert speaker's name] uses the non sequitur fallacy. [S/he] says, "Insert quotation." The conclusion that [insert conclusion] does not follow logically from the idea that supposedly supports it, that [insert faulty supporting idea]. [Explain in detail why the conclusion does not follow logically from the evidence].

### False Analogy
[Insert speaker's name] creates a false analogy. [S/he] says, "Insert quotation." Just because [first variable] and [second variable] are alike in some ways, in that they [explain how they are alike], it does not mean that they are alike in others. [Explain in detail how they are different].

### Either / Or
[Insert speaker's name] commits an either / or fallacy: "Insert quotation." [S/he] suggests that only two options exist: either [name first option], or [name second option]. In fact there are more: [give other options].

### Post Hoc
[Insert speaker's name] commits a post hoc fallacy: "Insert quotation." [S/he] assumes that because event A, [name event], came before event B, [name event], that therefore, event A caused event B. [Insert name] fails to show a causal relationship between [insert event A] and [insert event B], so [s/he] should not assume that the first event caused the second. [Provide detailed examples of other plausible causes].

### Abusive Ad Hominem
[Insert speaker's name] offers an ineffective rebuttal by employing an ad hominem fallacy. [S/he] states, "Insert quotation." [Insert speaker's name] attacks [name the person being attacked] by [explain the form of the attack] instead of focusing on the issue, [name the issue]. The fact that [name the person being attacked] [point out negative trait] does not invalidate [his / her] argument.

**Template Tip**

Avoid using contractions (i.e., don't, won't, can't shouldn't) in formal writing. If you borrow language from the quotation in your analysis, remove the contraction or put quotation marks around the word. Do not change the contraction inside of the quotation marks.

*STEP 2*: write a creative title._____

*STEP 3*: choose the correct template from the previous page and write a paragraph.

_____

_____

_____

_____

_____

_____

_____

_____

_____

_____

_____

_____

_____

_____

_____

_____

_____

_____

_____

# Exercise 36

**Dimsdale complained, "Ever since Rudi Galgudi moved in across the street, bad things have been happening in the neighborhood. He's got to be the cause!"**

*STEP 1: reconstruct the argument in standard form.*

Since (premise) _____,

_____,

Therefore (conclusion) _____.

## Templates

### Hasty Generalization

[Insert speaker's name] makes a hasty generalization: "Insert quotation." [Insert speaker's name] generalizes that [insert the generalization/conclusion] based on insufficient evidence, that [identify evidence/premise]; however, [explain why the particular "sample" does represent to the entire "population"].

### Non Sequitur

[Insert speaker's name] uses the non sequitur fallacy. [S/he] says, "Insert quotation." The conclusion that [insert conclusion] does not follow logically from the idea that supposedly supports it, that [insert faulty supporting idea]. [Explain in detail why the conclusion does not follow logically from the evidence].

### False Analogy

[Insert speaker's name] creates a false analogy. [S/he] says, "Insert quotation." Just because [first variable] and [second variable] are alike in some ways, in that they [explain how they are alike], it does not mean that they are alike in others. [Explain in detail how they are different].

### Either / Or

[Insert speaker's name] commits an either / or fallacy: "Insert quotation." [S/he] suggests that only two options exist: either [name first option], or [name second option]. In fact there are more: [give other options].

### Post Hoc

[Insert speaker's name] commits a post hoc fallacy: "Insert quotation." [S/he] assumes that because event A, [name event], came before event B, [name event], that therefore, event A caused event B. [Insert name] fails to show a causal relationship between [insert event A] and [insert event B], so [s/he] should not assume that the first event caused the second. [Provide detailed examples of other plausible causes].

### Abusive Ad Hominem

[Insert speaker's name] offers an ineffective rebuttal by employing an ad hominem fallacy. [S/he] states, "Insert quotation." [Insert speaker's name] attacks [name the person being attacked] by [explain the form of the attack] instead of focusing on the issue, [name the issue]. The fact that [name the person being attacked] [point out negative trait] does not invalidate [his / her] argument.

**STEP 2**: write a creative title._____

**STEP 3**: choose the correct template from the previous page and write a paragraph.

_____

_____

_____

_____

_____

_____

_____

_____

_____

_____

_____

_____

_____

_____

_____

_____

_____

_____

_____

_____

_____

**Exercise 37**

> **Guy Gullible said, "These faith healers really work! I seen one when I caught a cold and a week later I was feeling fine."**

*STEP 1*: *reconstruct the argument in standard form.*

Since (premise) _____,

_____,

Therefore (conclusion) _____.

## Templates

### Hasty Generalization
[Insert speaker's name] makes a hasty generalization: "Insert quotation." [Insert speaker's name] generalizes that [insert the generalization/conclusion] based on insufficient evidence, that [identify evidence/premise]; however, [explain why the particular "sample" does represent to the entire "population"].

### Non Sequitur
[Insert speaker's name] uses the non sequitur fallacy. [S/he] says, "Insert quotation." The conclusion that [insert conclusion] does not follow logically from the idea that supposedly supports it, that [insert faulty supporting idea]. [Explain in detail why the conclusion does not follow logically from the evidence].

### False Analogy
[Insert speaker's name] creates a false analogy. [S/he] says, "Insert quotation." Just because [first variable] and [second variable] are alike in some ways, in that they [explain how they are alike], it does not mean that they are alike in others. [Explain in detail how they are different].

### Either / Or
[Insert speaker's name] commits an either / or fallacy: "Insert quotation." [S/he] suggests that only two options exist: either [name first option], or [name second option]. In fact there are more: [give other options].

### Post Hoc
[Insert speaker's name] commits a post hoc fallacy: "Insert quotation." [S/he] assumes that because event A, [name event], came before event B, [name event], that therefore, event A caused event B. [Insert name] fails to show a causal relationship between [insert event A] and [insert event B], so [s/he] should not assume that the first event caused the second. [Provide detailed examples of other plausible causes].

### Abusive Ad Hominem
[Insert speaker's name] offers an ineffective rebuttal by employing an ad hominem fallacy. [S/he] states, "Insert quotation." [Insert speaker's name] attacks [name the person being attacked] by [explain the form of the attack] instead of focusing on the issue, [name the issue]. The fact that [name the person being attacked] [point out negative trait] does not invalidate [his / her] argument.

**STEP 2**: write a creative title._____

**STEP 3**: choose the correct template from the previous page and write a paragraph.

_____

_____

_____

_____

_____

_____

_____

_____

_____

_____

_____

_____

_____

_____

_____

_____

_____

_____

_____

_____

_____

_____

_____

**Exercise 38**

**Little Stanley Stinky sadly observed, "Either I take a shower or no one will go to the prom with me."**

*STEP 1*: reconstruct the argument in standard form.

Since (premise) _____,

and (implied premise) _____

Therefore (conclusion) _____.

## Templates

### Hasty Generalization
[Insert speaker's name] makes a hasty generalization: "Insert quotation." [Insert speaker's name] generalizes that [insert the generalization/conclusion] based on insufficient evidence, that [identify evidence/premise]; however, [explain why the particular "sample" does represent to the entire "population"].

### Non Sequitur
[Insert speaker's name] uses the non sequitur fallacy. [S/he] says, "Insert quotation." The conclusion that [insert conclusion] does not follow logically from the idea that supposedly supports it, that [insert faulty supporting idea]. [Explain in detail why the conclusion does not follow logically from the evidence].

### False Analogy
[Insert speaker's name] creates a false analogy. [S/he] says, "Insert quotation." Just because [first variable] and [second variable] are alike in some ways, in that they [explain how they are alike], it does not mean that they are alike in others. [Explain in detail how they are different].

### Either / Or
[Insert speaker's name] commits an either / or fallacy: "Insert quotation." [S/he] suggests that only two options exist: either [name first option], or [name second option]. In fact there are more: [give other options].

### Post Hoc
[Insert speaker's name] commits a post hoc fallacy: "Insert quotation." [S/he] assumes that because event A, [name event], came before event B, [name event], that therefore, event A caused event B. [Insert name] fails to show a causal relationship between [insert event A] and [insert event B], so [s/he] should not assume that the first event caused the second. [Provide detailed examples of other plausible causes].

### Abusive Ad Hominem
[Insert speaker's name] offers an ineffective rebuttal by employing an ad hominem fallacy. [S/he] states, "Insert quotation." [Insert speaker's name] attacks [name the person being attacked] by [explain the form of the attack] instead of focusing on the issue, [name the issue]. The fact that [name the person being attacked] [point out negative trait] does not invalidate [his / her] argument.

**Template Tip**

When citing a speaker or a writer, cite their entire name (e.g., Stanley Stinky) the first time you write it and then the last name "Stinky" for the rest of the paragraph. If you only have the first name just write the first name.

*STEP 2*: write a creative title._____

*STEP 3*: choose the correct template from the previous page and write a paragraph.

_____

_____

_____

_____

_____

_____

_____

_____

_____

_____

_____

_____

_____

_____

_____

_____

_____

_____

_____

_____

**Exercise 39**

### Beowulf noted, "Young Grendel does a lot of rap singing; he must be in a gang."

*STEP 1*: *reconstruct the argument in standard form.*

Since (premise) _____,

_____,

Therefore (conclusion) _____.

### Templates

**Hasty Generalization**

[Insert speaker's name] makes a hasty generalization: "Insert quotation." [Insert speaker's name] generalizes that [insert the generalization/conclusion] based on insufficient evidence, that [identify evidence/premise]; however, [explain why the particular "sample" does represent to the entire "population"].

**Non Sequitur**

[Insert speaker's name] uses the non sequitur fallacy. [S/he] says, "Insert quotation." The conclusion that [insert conclusion] does not follow logically from the idea that supposedly supports it, that [insert faulty supporting idea]. [Explain in detail why the conclusion does not follow logically from the evidence].

**False Analogy**

[Insert speaker's name] creates a false analogy. [S/he] says, "Insert quotation." Just because [first variable] and [second variable] are alike in some ways, in that they [explain how they are alike], it does not mean that they are alike in others. [Explain in detail how they are different].

**Either / Or**

[Insert speaker's name] commits an either / or fallacy: "Insert quotation." [S/he] suggests that only two options exist: either [name first option], or [name second option]. In fact there are more: [give other options].

**Post Hoc**

[Insert speaker's name] commits a post hoc fallacy: "Insert quotation." [S/he] assumes that because event A, [name event], came before event B, [name event], that therefore, event A caused event B. [Insert name] fails to show a causal relationship between [insert event A] and [insert event B], so [s/he] should not assume that the first event caused the second. [Provide detailed examples of other plausible causes].

**Abusive Ad Hominem**

[Insert speaker's name] offers an ineffective rebuttal by employing an ad hominem fallacy. [S/he] states, "Insert quotation." [Insert speaker's name] attacks [name the person being attacked] by [explain the form of the attack] instead of focusing on the issue, [name the issue]. The fact that [name the person being attacked] [point out negative trait] does not invalidate [his / her] argument.

***STEP 2***: *write a creative title.* _____

***STEP 3***: *choose the correct template from the previous page and write a paragraph.*

_____

_____

_____

_____

_____

_____

_____

_____

_____

_____

_____

_____

_____

_____

_____

_____

_____

_____

_____

_____

_____

## Exercise 40

**Ephedra says, "If my teacher Mr. Spear doesn't do any homework, I shouldn't have to do any!"**

*STEP 1*: *reconstruct the argument in standard form.*

Since (premise) _____,

_____,

Therefore (conclusion) _____.

### Templates

### Hasty Generalization

[Insert speaker's name] makes a hasty generalization: "Insert quotation." [Insert speaker's name] generalizes that [insert the generalization/conclusion] based on insufficient evidence, that [identify evidence/premise]; however, [explain why the particular "sample" does represent to the entire "population"].

### Non Sequitur

[Insert speaker's name] uses the non sequitur fallacy. [S/he] says, "Insert quotation." The conclusion that [insert conclusion] does not follow logically from the idea that supposedly supports it, that [insert faulty supporting idea]. [Explain in detail why the conclusion does not follow logically from the evidence].

### False Analogy

[Insert speaker's name] creates a false analogy. [S/he] says, "Insert quotation." Just because [first variable] and [second variable] are alike in some ways, in that they [explain how they are alike], it does not mean that they are alike in others. [Explain in detail how they are different].

### Either / Or

[Insert speaker's name] commits an either / or fallacy: "Insert quotation." [S/he] suggests that only two options exist: either [name first option], or [name second option]. In fact there are more: [give other options].

### Post Hoc

[Insert speaker's name] commits a post hoc fallacy: "Insert quotation." [S/he] assumes that because event A, [name event], came before event B, [name event], that therefore, event A caused event B. [Insert name] fails to show a causal relationship between [insert event A] and [insert event B], so [s/he] should not assume that the first event caused the second. [Provide detailed examples of other plausible causes].

### Abusive Ad Hominem

[Insert speaker's name] offers an ineffective rebuttal by employing an ad hominem fallacy. [S/he] states, "Insert quotation." [Insert speaker's name] attacks [name the person being attacked] by [explain the form of the attack] instead of focusing on the issue, [name the issue]. The fact that [name the person being attacked] [point out negative trait] does not invalidate [his / her] argument.

**STEP 2**: *write a creative title.* _____

**STEP 3**: *choose the correct template from the previous page and write a paragraph.*

_____

_____

_____

_____

_____

_____

_____

_____

_____

_____

_____

_____

_____

_____

_____

_____

_____

_____

_____

_____

_____

_____

_____

# PART 5
# WELCOME TO FALLACY MONGERVILLE

**Exercise 41**

**Tommy Morton noted, "The Bradford family is not very graceful. Little Billy Bradford dances like a real stiff!"**

*STEP 1*: *reconstruct the argument in standard form.*

Since (premise) _____,

Therefore (conclusion) _____.

*STEP 2*: *write an analytical paragraph.*

_____

_____

_____

_____

_____

_____

_____

_____

_____

_____

_____

_____

_____

_____

_____

_____

_____

# Exercise 42

**Towel Lou cried out, "Andy Dandy says we should have school uniforms, but do we want to take advice from a man who has the world's largest collection of dolls?"**

*STEP 1*: reconstruct the argument in standard form.

Since (premise) _____,

Therefore (conclusion) _____.

*STEP 2*: write an analytical paragraph.

_____

_____

_____

_____

_____

_____

_____

_____

_____

_____

_____

_____

_____

_____

_____

_____

_____

_____

_____

## Exercise 43

**Coach Testosterone screamed, "An athlete is an athlete. So if professional athletes take steroids, then Ludville Jr. High School athletes should be able to take them too."**

*STEP 1*: *reconstruct the argument in standard form.*

Since (premise) _____,

Therefore (conclusion) _____.

*STEP 2*: *write an analytical paragraph.*

_____

_____

_____

_____

_____

_____

_____

_____

_____

_____

_____

_____

_____

_____

_____

_____

_____

_____

## Exercise 44

**Dr. Funzit said, "Eulogy got skin cancer after she got an eagle tattoo on her back. It just goes to show you that eagle tattoos cause cancer.**

*STEP 1*: reconstruct the argument in standard form.

Since (premise) _____ ,

Therefore (conclusion) _____ .

*STEP 2*: write an analytical paragraph.

_____

_____

_____

_____

_____

_____

_____

_____

_____

_____

_____

_____

_____

_____

_____

_____

_____

_____

_____

**Exercise 45**

**Jane reasoned, "Gary must be part monkey; he loves to eat bananas."**

*STEP 1*: *reconstruct the argument in standard form.*

Since (premise) _____,

and (implied premise) _____

Therefore (conclusion) _____.

*STEP 2*: *write an analytical paragraph.*

_____

_____

_____

_____

_____

_____

_____

_____

_____

_____

_____

_____

_____

_____

_____

_____

_____

_____

_____

## Exercise 46

**Slothman said, "I think I'm allergic to work. Last Saturday, after my dad made me mow the lawn, I got a sick feeling in my stomach."**

*STEP 1*: reconstruct the argument in standard form.

Since (premise) _____,

Therefore (conclusion) _____.

*STEP 2*: write an analytical paragraph.

_____

_____

_____

_____

_____

_____

_____

_____

_____

_____

_____

_____

_____

_____

_____

_____

_____

_____

_____

_____

## Exercise 47

**The frightened students of Ludville Jr. High reasoned, "Mrs. Gruff was a drill sergeant in the Marine Corp. She is going to be one mean Vice Principal!"**

*STEP 1*: reconstruct the argument in standard form.

Since (premise) _____ ,

Therefore (conclusion) _____ .

*STEP 2*: write an analytical paragraph.

_____

_____

_____

_____

_____

_____

_____

_____

_____

_____

_____

_____

_____

_____

_____

_____

_____

# PART 6
# FALLACY ESSAYS

# Argument 1

What a Wonderful Woman's World

Mina Menhaden, Ph. D, University of Ludville

Men are savages. Look at Adolph Hitler and Attila the Hun--savages! Women don't need men to provide for them anymore. Either men shape up, or they will find themselves alone. Joe Macho says men should act like men and take charge, but he's a stupid man. So of course he would say that. Women need to realize that the struggle for equality is a war, and they have to fight like it's a war. The world is in a mess today. This is because for thousands of years men have been calling the shots. Women carry babies for nine months; they have earned the right to be in charge. Therefore, women need to be in charge of the world!

Directions: identify the six fallacies

1. "Men are savages. Look at Adolph Hitler and Attila the Hun--savages!"

   This argument is a _____ fallacy.

2. "Either men shape up, or they will find themselves alone."

   This argument is an _____ fallacy.

3. "Joe Macho says men should act like men and take charge, but he's a stupid man. So of course he would say that."

   This argument is an _____ fallacy.

4. "Women need to realize that the struggle for equality is a war. And they have to fight like it's a war."

   This argument is a _____ fallacy.

5. "The world is in a mess today. This is because for thousands of years men have been calling the shots."

   This argument is a _____ fallacy.

6. "Women carry babies for nine months; they have earned the right to be in charge."

   This argument is a _____ fallacy.

CONCLUSION: put women in charge of the world!

# Standard Form

Directions: construct the fallacies in standard form.

1. _____ fallacy

   Since (premise) _____,

   Therefore (conclusion) _____.

2. _____ fallacy

   Since (premise) _____,

   and (implied premise) _____

   Therefore (conclusion) _____.

3. _____ fallacy

   Since (premise) _____,

   Therefore (conclusion) _____.

4. _____ fallacy

   Since (premise) _____,

   Therefore (conclusion) _____.

5. _____ fallacy

   Since (premise) _____,

   Therefore (conclusion) _____.

6. _____ fallacy

   Since (premise) _____,

   Therefore (conclusion) _____.

# Building a Thesis

Step one: generate a conclusion refuting the author's argument.

(The conclusion is the thesis.)

THESIS TEMPLATE:   In "[insert title of the essay]," [insert full name of the author], fails to argue logically that [insert author's conclusion].


EXAMPLE:        In "**What a Wonderful Woman's World**," **Mina Menhaden** fails to argue logically that **women should rule the world**.


Step two: Generate the premises that support your conclusion.

PREMISE TEMPLATE: [Insert author's last name] commits many fallacies.

EXAMPLE:   **Menhaden** commits many fallacies.


These two statements make up the thesis. Write the thesis as one or two sentences:

Two sentences:     In "What a Wonderful Woman's World," Mina Menhaden fails to argue logically that women should rule the world. Menhaden commits many fallacies.


One sentence with the word "because" added.

In "What a Wonderful Woman's World," Mina Menhaden fails to argue logically that women should rule the world because Menhaden commits many fallacies.

*Sample Essay (MLA)*

Stewart Pidd

Professor Pimple

English 110

5 November 2005

Positions of Authority

Traditionally, women have been responsible for the household and the family, but times have changed and with this change so have the roles that women can play in a complex technological society. One can reasonably argue that tradition should not prevent talented women from holding positions of power. In "What a Woman's World," Mina Menhaden fails to effectively argue that women should be in charge because she commits many fallacies.

Menhaden begins by committing a hasty generalization fallacy: she says, "Men are savages. Look at Adolph Hitler and Attila the Hun--savages!" Menhaden generalizes that men are uncivilized based on the insufficient evidence, that Hitler and Attila the Hun were savages; however, Hitler and Hun are only two men. Their brutal behavior does not represent the behavior of all men.

Next, Menhaden creates a non sequitur fallacy. She writes, "Women carry babies for nine months; they have earned the right to be in charge." The conclusion that women should be in charge does not follow logically from the idea that supposedly supports it, that women carry babies for nine months. The fact that women have children does not entitle them to positions of authority. A woman's leadership skills, not her biology, will determine whether or not she is an effective leader.

After committing the non sequitur, Menhaden creates a false analogy. "Women have to realize the struggle for equality is a war. And they have to fight like it's a war." Just because fighting in a war and trying to gain equality are alike in some ways, in that they both involve struggle and an objective to achieve, it does not mean that they are alike in others. In war, problems are solved through violence and destruction. The fight for equality is a social issue that should be resolved through appropriate legislation.

Menhaden also forms an either / or fallacy: "Women don't need men to provide for them anymore. Either men shape up, or they will find themselves alone." She suggests that only two options exist: men can shape up or they can be alone. In fact there are more: men and women can first appreciate each other's differences and then work together for a reasonable compromise.

Next, Menhaden commits a post hoc fallacy: "The world is in a mess. This is because for thousands of years men have been calling the shots." She assumes that because event A, the thousands of years that men have been holding positions of power, came before event B, the current chaotic state of the world, that therefore, event A caused event B. Menhaden fails to show a causal relationship, so she should not assume that the first event caused the second. The world is a complex place. Other factors besides men contribute to its volatile condition.

Lastly, Menhaden offers an ineffective rebuttal by employing an ad hominem fallacy. She states, "Joe Macho says men should act like men and take charge, but he's a stupid man. So of course he would say that." Menhaden attacks Joe Macho by calling him a stupid man, instead focusing on the issue, who should be in charge of the world.

Menhaden's conclusion that women should be in charge could be correct. She fails, however, to provide any valid reasons to support that conclusion. She could strengthen her arguments by providing more relevant, sufficient and acceptable premises to help support the idea that women should assume leadership roles.

# Argument 2

## Joe Macho's Rebuttal
## Joseph Macho, Owner Macho's Bar & Grill

Yo, I just heard about an article by this gal Dr. "Man Hater." So she thinks that women should be in charge, eh? [Well, she is just an uptight nerd with a Playa Hater Degree who reads and talks too much and couldn't get a date on a Saturday night even if she paid someone. She is the last person we should be listening to.]

[The truth be known, women ain't never satisfied. When I was young and stupid, I tried to do whatever my first wife wanted, but it was never good enough.] Looking back on it now, [the fact that I wasn't mean enough caused her to leave!] It's clear to me now that [you gotta either be a jerk and show them women who's boss or you are doomed to a life of mini vans and soccer practice.] [The reality is the man is the king of the household; therefore everyone else should serve him as if he were royalty.] I know that for sure. [Need more proof that men need to be in charge? You see my chopper here? I don't think I need to say anything more.]

CONCLUSION: men should be in charge.

# Standard Form

Directions: construct the fallacies in standard form.

1. _____ fallacy

    Since (premise) _____,

    Therefore (conclusion) _____.

2. _____ fallacy

    Since (premise) _____,

    Therefore (conclusion) _____.

3. _____ fallacy

    Since (premise) _____,

    Therefore (conclusion) _____.

4. _____ fallacy

    Since (premise) _____,

    and (implied premise) _____

    Therefore (conclusion) _____.

5. _____ fallacy

    Since (premise) _____,

    Therefore (conclusion) _____.

6. _____ fallacy

    Since (premise) _____,

    Therefore (conclusion) _____.

Directions: write out an analytical paragraph for each fallacy.

## Abusive Ad Hominem

_____

_____

_____

_____

_____

_____

_____

_____

_____

_____

_____

_____

_____

_____

## Hasty Generalization

_____

_____

_____

_____

_____

_____

_____

_____

_____

_____

_____

_____

_____

_____

_____

# Post Hoc

# Either / Or

# False Analogy

_____
_____
_____
_____
_____
_____
_____
_____
_____
_____
_____
_____
_____
_____
_____
_____
_____
_____

# Non Sequitur

_____
_____
_____
_____
_____
_____
_____
_____
_____
_____
_____
_____
_____
_____
_____

# Peer Review Checklist

Directions: circle YES or NO for each question and mark all errors on the actual essay.

1. Does the writer use the correct MLA or APA style?   YES / NO

2. Is the title creative?   YES / NO

## Introductory Paragraph

1. Does the writer begin with general background information?   YES / NO

2. Has the writer ended the introduction with a thesis that includes a premise and a conclusion?   YES / NO

> THESIS TEMPLATE: In "[insert title of the essay]," [insert full name of the author] fails to argue logically that [insert author's conclusion]. [Insert author's last name] commits many fallacies.

## Body Paragraphs

### Abusive Ad Hominem

1. Does the paragraph begin with a correctly formatted claim?   YES / NO

2. Is the quoted evidence the ad hominem fallacy?   YES / NO

3. Is the quotation punctuated correctly?   YES / NO

4. Has the writer used the ad hominem template?   YES / NO

5. Does the author specifically identify the form of the attack?   YES / NO

### Hasty Generalization

1. Does the paragraph begin with a correctly formatted claim?   YES / NO

**[Author's last name] makes a hasty generalization:**

2. Is the quoted evidence actually the hasty generalization?   YES / NO

3. Is the quotation punctuated correctly?   YES / NO

4. Has the writer used the hasty generalization template?   YES / NO

5. Does the writer correctly identify the premise (the evidence) and conclusion (the generalization)?   YES / NO

6. Does the writer explain specifically why the evidence is insufficient?   YES / NO

### Post Hoc

1. Does the paragraph begin with a correctly formatted claim?   YES / NO

2. Is the quoted evidence the actual post hoc fallacy?   YES / NO

3. Is the quotation punctuated correctly?   YES / NO

4. Has the writer used the post hoc template?   YES / NO

5. Does the writer identify the premise and conclusion?   YES / NO

6. In the templates, are events A and B written as noun phrases and not sentences?   YES / NO

**Either / Or**

| | |
|---|---|
| 1. Does the paragraph begin with a correctly formatted claim? | YES / NO |
| 2. Is the quoted evidence the actual either / or fallacy? | YES / NO |
| 3. Is the quotation punctuated correctly? | YES / NO |
| 4. Has the writer used the either / or template? | YES / NO |
| 5. Are the options in the template parallel? | YES / NO |
| 6. Does the writer give reasonable and specific alternatives? | YES / NO |

**False Analogy**

| | |
|---|---|
| 1. Does the paragraph begin with a correctly formatted claim? | YES / NO |
| 2. Is the quoted evidence the false analogy? | YES / NO |
| 3. Is the quotation punctuated correctly? | YES / NO |
| 4. Has the writer used the false analogy template? | YES / NO |
| 5. Does the writer correctly identify the premise and conclusion? | YES / NO |
| 6. Has the writer used parallel structure? | YES / NO |

**Non Sequitur**

| | |
|---|---|
| 1. Does the paragraph begin with a correctly formatted claim? | YES / NO |
| 2. Is the quoted evidence the non sequitur? | YES / NO |
| 3. Is the quotation punctuated correctly? | YES / NO |
| 4. Has the writer used the non sequitur template? | YES / NO |
| 5. Does the writer correctly identify the premise and conclusion? | YES / NO |
| 6. Does the writer explain in detail why the premise does not support the conclusion? | YES / NO |

### Concluding Paragraph

| | |
|---|---|
| 1. Has the writer avoided writing "In conclusion"? | YES / NO |
| 2. Does the writer paraphrase the thesis? | YES / NO |
| 3. Does the writer explain how to strengthen the fallacious argument? | YES / NO |

**Miscellaneous**

| | |
|---|---|
| 1. Has the writer avoided using quotations in the commentary sections? | YES / NO |
| 2. Has the writer avoided using contractions? | YES / NO |
| 3. Has the writer avoided using the pronouns "I," "me," "we," "our," "you," "your"? | YES / NO |

Argument 3

## The Onionator
### Curly Von Onionstien

As governor of this fine state, my first course of business will be to overhaul the ailing health insurance industry. My opponent says my proposal to fix this problem would hurt the elderly because it calls for an increase in their health premiums. [Of course she'd put down my policy: she's eighty-seven years old. As usual, she's just looking out for number one.]

My opponent also attacks my lack of experience as a politician. What she doesn't tell you is that I have been working in the business world for 23 years. [If I can run a fortune 500 company, I should be able to run a state government.] Before I was a businessman, [I was a Chicago pool shark, so it follows that I will make a great governor.]

[Many people don't know this, but after the current governor took office, the unemployment level shot up by twenty percent. She has really made a mess of our industrial base.] [Jobs are leaving the state at an alarming rate. In my hometown of Ludville they lost ten businesses in the last month.] In the final analysis [it seems like there are only two choices: either you choose me for governor or you plan on things getting worse in the state.]

CONCLUSION: voters should elect Curly Von Onionstien for Governor!

# Standard Form

<u>Directions</u>: construct the fallacies in standard form.

1. _____ fallacy

   Since (premise) _____,

   Therefore (conclusion) _____.


2. _____ fallacy

   Since (premise) _____,

   Therefore (conclusion) _____.


3. _____ fallacy

   Since (premise) _____,

   Therefore (conclusion) _____.


4. _____ fallacy

   Since (premise) _____,

   Therefore (conclusion) _____.


5. _____ fallacy

   Since (premise) _____,

   Therefore (conclusion) _____.


6. _____ fallacy

   Since (premise) _____,

   and (implied premise) _____

   Therefore (conclusion) _____.

Directions: write out an analytical paragraph for each fallacy.

## Abusive Ad Hominem

_____
_____
_____
_____
_____
_____
_____
_____
_____
_____
_____
_____
_____
_____

## False Analogy

_____
_____
_____
_____
_____
_____
_____
_____
_____
_____
_____
_____
_____
_____
_____

# Non Sequitur

_____

_____

_____

_____

_____

_____

_____

_____

_____

_____

_____

_____

_____

# Post Hoc

_____

_____

_____

_____

_____

_____

_____

_____

_____

_____

_____

_____

_____

Hasty Generalization

_____
_____
_____
_____
_____
_____
_____
_____
_____
_____
_____
_____
_____
_____

Either / Or

_____
_____
_____
_____
_____
_____
_____
_____
_____
_____
_____
_____
_____
_____

# Peer Review Checklist

Directions: circle YES or NO for each question and mark all errors on the actual essay.

1. Does the writer use the correct MLA or APA style?  YES / NO

2. Is the title creative?  YES / NO

## Introductory Paragraph

1. Does the writer begin with general background information?  YES / NO

2. Has the writer ended the introduction with a thesis that includes a premise and a conclusion?  YES / NO

> THESIS TEMPLATE: In "[insert title of the essay]," [insert full name of the author] fails to argue logically that [insert author's conclusion]. [Insert author's last name] commits many fallacies.

## Body Paragraphs

### Abusive Ad Hominem

1. Does the paragraph begin with a correctly formatted claim?  YES / NO

2. Is the quoted evidence the ad hominem fallacy?  YES / NO

3. Is the quotation punctuated correctly?  YES / NO

4. Has the writer used the ad hominem template?  YES / NO

5. Does the author specifically identify the form of the attack?  YES / NO

### False Analogy

1. Does the paragraph begin with a correctly formatted claim?  YES / NO

2. Is the quoted evidence the false analogy?  YES / NO

3. Is the quotation punctuated correctly?  YES / NO

4. Has the writer used the false analogy template?  YES / NO

5. Does the writer correctly identify the premise and conclusion?  YES / NO

6. Has the writer used parallel structure?  YES / NO

### Non Sequitur

1. Does the paragraph begin with a correctly formatted claim?  YES / NO

2. Is the quoted evidence the non sequitur?  YES / NO

3. Is the quotation punctuated correctly?  YES / NO

4. Has the writer used the non sequitur template?  YES / NO

5. Does the writer correctly identify the premise and conclusion?  YES / NO

6. Does the writer explain in detail why the premise does not support the conclusion?  YES / NO

## Post Hoc

1. Does the paragraph begin with a correctly formatted claim?          YES / NO
2. Is the quoted evidence the actual post hoc fallacy?          YES / NO
3. Is the quotation punctuated correctly?          YES / NO
4. Has the writer used the post hoc template?          YES / NO
5. Does the writer identify the premise and conclusion?          YES / NO
6. In the templates, are events A and B written as noun phrases and not sentences?

          YES / NO

## Hasty Generalization

1. Does the paragraph begin with a correctly formatted claim?          YES / NO

   **[Author's last name] makes a hasty generalization:**

2. Is the quoted evidence actually the hasty generalization?          YES / NO
3. Is the quotation punctuated correctly?          YES / NO
4. Has the writer used the hasty generalization template?          YES / NO
5. Does the writer correctly identify the premise (the evidence)
   and conclusion (the generalization)?          YES / NO
6. Does the writer explain specifically why the evidence is insufficient?          YES / NO

## Either / Or

1. Does the paragraph begin with a correctly formatted claim?          YES / NO
2. Is the quoted evidence the actual either / or fallacy?          YES / NO
3. Is the quotation punctuated correctly?          YES / NO
4. Has the writer used the either / or template?          YES / NO
5. Are the options in the template parallel?          YES / NO
6. Does the writer give reasonable and specific alternatives?          YES / NO

### Concluding Paragraph

1. Has the writer avoided writing "In conclusion"?          YES / NO
2. Does the writer paraphrase the thesis?          YES / NO
3. Does the writer explain how to strengthen the fallacious argument?          YES / NO

## Miscellaneous

1. Has the writer avoided using quotations in the commentary sections?          YES / NO
2. Has the writer avoided using contractions?          YES / NO
3. Has the writer avoided using the pronouns "I," "me," "we," "our," "you," "your"?          YES / NO

Argument 4

## American Cockroach
### Zlyn Zlang

I know that this idea might seem strange at first, but if you look at it logically, you will see that it makes perfect sense. My biggest detractor, Mr. Bigmouth, constantly criticizes my proposal, citing health risks involved in eating cockroaches. Of course he would have this view. Hello? Has everyone forgotten that he is the money-grubbing CEO of Cockroach Killers Unlimited, a pest control conglomerate? Look people, an organism is an organism. Eating roaches is like eating beef or chicken. These delicious creatures are here for us to enjoy. Moreover, cockroaches are a good source of potassium. So you need to eat some regularly, or you'll find yourself deficient in this vital mineral. The simple fact is that cockroaches are healthy to eat. I eat them everyday, and I enjoy perfect health. Insects are high in protein, so eating cockroaches would be an easy way to stay on a low-carb diet. Finally, eating cockroaches has brought me great luck. Yesterday, right after I found some in my trash and ate them, I won the lottery. Therefore, my advice is simple: eat up, America!

CONCLUSION: Americans need to eat more cockroaches.

# Standard Form

Directions: construct the fallacies in standard form.

1. _____ fallacy

   Since (premise) _____,

   Therefore (conclusion) _____.


2. _____ fallacy

   Since (premise) _____,

   Therefore (conclusion) _____.


3. _____ fallacy

   Since (premise) _____,

   and (implied premise) _____

   Therefore (conclusion) _____.


4. _____ fallacy

   Since (premise) _____,

   Therefore (conclusion) _____.


5. _____ fallacy

   Since (premise) _____,

   Therefore (conclusion) _____.


6. _____ fallacy

   Since (premise) _____,

   Therefore (conclusion) _____.

Directions: write out an analytical paragraph for each fallacy.

## Abusive Ad Hominem

_____
_____
_____
_____
_____
_____
_____
_____
_____
_____
_____
_____
_____
_____
_____

## False Analogy

_____
_____
_____
_____
_____
_____
_____
_____
_____
_____
_____
_____
_____
_____
_____
_____
_____

# Either / Or

_____

_____

_____

_____

_____

_____

_____

_____

_____

_____

_____

_____

_____

_____

_____

# Hasty Generalization

_____

_____

_____

_____

_____

_____

_____

_____

_____

_____

_____

_____

_____

_____

# Non Sequitur

_____
_____
_____
_____
_____
_____
_____
_____
_____
_____
_____
_____
_____
_____

# Post Hoc

_____
_____
_____
_____
_____
_____
_____
_____
_____
_____
_____
_____
_____
_____

# Peer Review Checklist

<u>Directions</u>: circle YES or NO for each question and mark all errors on the actual essay.

1. Does the writer use the correct MLA or APA style?                    YES / NO

2. Is the title creative?                                               YES / NO

## Introductory Paragraph

1. Does the writer begin with general background information?           YES / NO

2. Has the writer ended the introduction with a thesis that includes
   a premise and a conclusion?                                          YES / NO

> THESIS TEMPLATE: In "[insert title of the essay]," [insert full name of the author] fails to argue logically that [insert author's conclusion]. [Insert author's last name] commits many fallacies.

## Body Paragraphs

### Abusive Ad Hominem

1. Does the paragraph begin with a correctly formatted claim?          YES / NO

2. Is the quoted evidence the ad hominem fallacy?                       YES / NO

3. Is the quotation punctuated correctly?                               YES / NO

4. Has the writer used the ad hominem template?                        YES / NO

5. Does the author specifically identify the form of the attack?       YES / NO

### False Analogy

1. Does the paragraph begin with a correctly formatted claim?          YES / NO

2. Is the quoted evidence the false analogy?                           YES / NO

3. Is the quotation punctuated correctly?                              YES / NO

4. Has the writer used the false analogy template?                     YES / NO

5. Does the writer correctly identify the premise and conclusion?      YES / NO

6. Has the writer used parallel structure?                             YES / NO

### Either / Or

1. Does the paragraph begin with a correctly formatted claim?          YES / NO

2. Is the quoted evidence the actual either / or fallacy?              YES / NO

3. Is the quotation punctuated correctly?                              YES / NO

4. Has the writer used the either / or template?                      YES / NO

5. Are the options in the template parallel?                          YES / NO

6. Does the writer give reasonable and specific alternatives?         YES / NO

## Hasty Generalization

1. Does the paragraph begin with a correctly formatted claim?    YES / NO

**[Author's last name] makes a hasty generalization:**

2. Is the quoted evidence actually the hasty generalization?    YES / NO

3. Is the quotation punctuated correctly?    YES / NO

4. Has the writer used the hasty generalization template?    YES / NO

5. Does the writer correctly identify the premise (the evidence)
   and conclusion (the generalization)?    YES / NO

6. Does the writer explain specifically why the evidence is insufficient?    YES / NO

## Non Sequitur

1. Does the paragraph begin with a correctly formatted claim?    YES / NO

2. Is the quoted evidence the non sequitur?    YES / NO

3. Is the quotation punctuated correctly?    YES / NO

4. Has the writer used the non sequitur template?    YES / NO

5. Does the writer correctly identify the premise and conclusion?    YES / NO

6. Does the writer explain in detail why the premise does not support the conclusion?

YES / NO

## Post Hoc

1. Does the paragraph begin with a correctly formatted claim?    YES / NO

2. Is the quoted evidence the actual post hoc fallacy?    YES / NO

3. Is the quotation punctuated correctly?    YES / NO

4. Has the writer used the post hoc template?    YES / NO

5. Does the writer identify the premise and conclusion?    YES / NO

6. In the templates, are events A and B written as noun phrases and not sentences?

YES / NO

## Concluding Paragraph

1. Has the writer avoided writing "In conclusion"?    YES / NO

2. Does the writer paraphrase the thesis?    YES / NO

3. Does the writer explain how to strengthen the fallacious argument?    YES / NO

## Miscellaneous

1. Has the writer avoided using quotations in the commentary sections?    YES / NO

2. Has the writer avoided using contractions?    YES / NO

3. Has the writer avoided using the pronouns "I," "me," "we," "our," "you," "your"?    YES / NO

# Argument 5

## Get to Work, Kids!
## Olden Kidcrusher

Working hard at a young age makes for a successful adult. Curly Onionstien started working at the age of five, and he went on to become a very successful politician.

I don't know why all the bleeding hearts are getting so upset by my proposal. It is not secret that kids are capable of playing from dusk 'til dawn. They get up early and play, play, play. Surely, if kids can play then they can work.

Kids should shoulder some of the burden they place on the state. With a 30 billion dollar deficit, the state is in real trouble; it is obvious that only two choices exist: put kids to work or plunge the state deeper into debt and lose the way of life we all love.

I know this idea is controversial. In the last six months, child advocates, parents, and school administrators have all come out against my proposal. But who are they to put my ideas down? Look at the terrible job they have done with our children.

Few people would argue that kids were more respectful in the old days. Do you think it's any coincidence that after kids enter the workforce they become respectful? Am I the only one who sees the causal relationship between kids working and being respectful?

In the final analysis, since America is a global super-power; it only seems reasonable that young people put on their work clothes and get busy! The factories of America are waiting, kids!

CONCLUSION: starting from kindergarten, kids should work to pay for their schooling.

# Standard Form

Directions: construct the fallacies in standard form.

1. _____ fallacy

   Since (premise) _____,

   Therefore (conclusion) _____.


2. _____ fallacy

   Since (premise) _____,

   Therefore (conclusion) _____.


3. _____ fallacy

   Since (premise) _____,

   and (implied premise) _____

   Therefore (conclusion) _____.


4. _____ fallacy

   Since (premise) _____,

   Therefore (conclusion) _____.


5. _____ fallacy

   Since (premise) _____,

   Therefore (conclusion) _____.


6. _____ fallacy

   Since (premise) _____,

   Therefore (conclusion) _____.

Directions: write out an analytical paragraph for each fallacy.

## Hasty Generalization

_____
_____
_____
_____
_____
_____
_____
_____
_____
_____
_____
_____
_____

## False Analogy

_____
_____
_____
_____
_____
_____
_____
_____
_____
_____
_____
_____
_____
_____
_____
_____
_____

## Abusive Ad Hominem

## Post Hoc

___

## Non Sequitur

___

# Peer Review Checklist

<u>Directions</u>: circle YES or NO for each question and mark all errors on the actual essay.

1. Does the writer use the correct MLA or APA style?                    YES / NO

2. Is the title creative?                                              YES / NO

## Introductory Paragraph

1. Does the writer begin with general background information?           YES / NO

2. Has the writer ended the introduction with a thesis that includes
   a premise and a conclusion?                                         YES / NO

> THESIS TEMPLATE: In "[insert title of the essay]," [insert full name of the author] fails to argue logically that [insert author's conclusion]. [Insert author's last name] commits many fallacies.

## Body Paragraphs

### Hasty Generalization

1. Does the paragraph begin with a correctly formatted claim?           YES / NO

   **[Author's last name] makes a hasty generalization:**

2. Is the quoted evidence actually the hasty generalization?            YES / NO

3. Is the quotation punctuated correctly?                              YES / NO

4. Has the writer used the hasty generalization template?              YES / NO

5. Does the writer correctly identify the premise (the evidence)
   and conclusion (the generalization)?                               YES / NO

6. Does the writer explain specifically why the evidence is insufficient?  YES / NO


### False Analogy

1. Does the paragraph begin with a correctly formatted claim?           YES / NO

2. Is the quoted evidence the false analogy?                           YES / NO

3. Is the quotation punctuated correctly?                              YES / NO

4. Has the writer used the false analogy template?                     YES / NO

5. Does the writer correctly identify the premise and conclusion?       YES / NO

6. Has the writer used parallel structure?                             YES / NO


### Either / Or

1. Does the paragraph begin with a correctly formatted claim?           YES / NO

2. Is the quoted evidence the actual either / or fallacy?               YES / NO

3. Is the quotation punctuated correctly?                              YES / NO

4. Has the writer used the either / or template?                       YES / NO

5. Are the options in the template parallel?                           YES / NO

6. Does the writer give reasonable and specific alternatives?           YES / NO

## Ad Hominem

| | |
|---|---|
| 1. Does the paragraph begin with a correctly formatted claim? | YES / NO |
| 2. Is the quoted evidence the ad hominem fallacy? | YES / NO |
| 3. Is the quotation punctuated correctly? | YES / NO |
| 4. Has the writer used the ad hominem template? | YES / NO |
| 5. Does the author specifically identify the form of the attack? | YES / NO |

## Post Hoc

| | |
|---|---|
| 1. Does the paragraph begin with a correctly formatted claim? | YES / NO |
| 2. Is the quoted evidence the actual post hoc fallacy? | YES / NO |
| 3. Is the quotation punctuated correctly? | YES / NO |
| 4. Has the writer used the post hoc template? | YES / NO |
| 5. Does the writer identify the premise and conclusion? | YES / NO |
| 6. In the templates, are events A and B written as noun phrases and not sentences? | YES / NO |

## Non Sequitur

| | |
|---|---|
| 1. Does the paragraph begin with a correctly formatted claim? | YES / NO |
| 2. Is the quoted evidence the non sequitur? | YES / NO |
| 3. Is the quotation punctuated correctly? | YES / NO |
| 4. Has the writer used the non sequitur template? | YES / NO |
| 5. Does the writer correctly identify the premise and conclusion? | YES / NO |
| 6. Does the writer explain in detail why the premise does not support the conclusion? | YES / NO |

## Concluding Paragraph

| | |
|---|---|
| 1. Has the writer avoided writing "In conclusion"? | YES / NO |
| 2. Does the writer paraphrase the thesis? | YES / NO |
| 3. Does the writer explain how to strengthen the fallacious argument? | YES / NO |

## Miscellaneous

| | |
|---|---|
| 1. Has the writer avoided using quotations in the commentary sections? | YES / NO |
| 2. Has the writer avoided using contractions? | YES / NO |
| 3. Has the writer avoided using the pronouns "I," "me," "we," "our," "you," "your"? | YES / NO |

# TIPS FOR TITLES

# Titles

**CAPITALIZATION**

For MLA style, always capitalize the first and last word of your title. Nouns, verbs, adjectives and adverbs should be capitalized. Articles (a, an, the), prepositions (from, of, to, into, at), and coordinating conjunctions (but, and) are not capitalized unless they are the first or last word of the title.

<u>Directions</u>: rewrite the following titles using the proper rules for capitalization.

1. the lottery _____ *The Lottery* _____

2. of mice and men_____

3. from here to eternity_____

4. into the great wide open_____

5. to the light house_____

6. as you like it _____

7. where it's at _____

8. boot camp for your brain _____

9. stairway to heaven _____

10. on the interpretation of dreams_____

Do not use **bold**, *italics*, <u>underlining</u>, or "quotation marks" in the title.

Avoid using "quotation marks" around your title.
   ***WRONG***: "The Hungry Chef"

Avoid <u>underlining</u> your title.
   ***WRONG***: <u>The Hungry Chef</u>

Avoid using **bold** in your title.
   ***WRONG***: **The Hungry Chef**

# Tips for Titles

## Using Literary Devices and Grammatical Phrases to Craft Creative Titles

A good title helps to establish the topic and tone of an essay. Most students, however, write boring, vague titles like "Essay # 3," "Midterm Exam," and "Gun Control." You can make a positive first impression on the reader with a good title.

Effective titles will contain literary devices (identifiable elements of literature) or different types of grammatical phrases. You can practice generating titles by working with these literary devices and phrases.

## Prepositional Phrases

A **prepositional phrase** is made up of a preposition (under, after, before, to, on, beneath) followed by a noun, a noun phrase, or a pronoun. Prepositional phrases point things out in a sentence, usually where something is or when something is taking place.

Directions: add an object.

1. After the _Gold Rush_

2. Under the _Overpass_

3. Beneath the _____

4. On the _____

5. Beyond the _____

6. By the _____

7. Into the _____

8. Inside the _____

9. From _____ to _____

Directions: add a preposition.

10. _____ the lighthouse

11. _____ my heart

12. _____ the River

13. _____ the Light of the Moon

14. _____ to Shining Sea

# Present Participles

A present participle is just an –ing verb (kicking, shouting).

> Runn<u>ing</u> on Empty

> Go<u>ing</u> to Chicago

<u>Directions</u>: fill in the blanks to create verb phrases.

1. Running _____ Down A Dream _____

2. Standing _____ On the Toes of Giants _____

3. Find_____ Nemo

4. Sleeping with _____

5. Waiting for _____

6. Smelling _____

7. _____ Flirt _____ing _____

8. _____ing _____

9. _____ing _____

10. _____ing _____

# Alliteration

Alliteration is the repetition of initial consonant sounds.

> <u>D</u>uane's <u>D</u>epressed

> <u>S</u>ong of the <u>S</u>outh

<u>Directions</u>: generate your own titles using alliteration.

1. The _____ Dirty _____ Dog

2. Melville's M_____

3. B_____ B_____ Bull

4. R_____ R_____

5. A_____ A_____ A_____ A_____

6. _____

# Twist a Familiar Saying

You can create good titles by changing some of the words in preexisting titles, sayings, or phrases. Replace the words "win" and "influence" with "lose" and "alienate" in the title *How to win Friends and Influence People,"* and you get *How to Lose Friends and Alienate People,* which is a funny title. Change the word "gorillas" to "guerillas" in the title *Gorillas in the Mist* and you get *Guerillas in the Mist,* which can mean something completely different than the original title.

<u>Directions</u>: twist the following titles and sayings:

1. Rome Wasn't Built in a Day

    Rome Wasn't _____**Destroyed**_____ in a Day

2. Every Cloud has a Silver Lining

    Every Cloud has a _____ Underlining

3. If at First You Don't Succeed, Try, Try Again

    If at First You Don't Succeed, _____ Up

4. Star Wars

    Car _____

5. Charlotte's Web

    Charlotte' s Web _____

6. Look Before You Leap

    _____ Before You Look

7. You Can't Judge a Book by Its Cover

    You _____ Judge a Book by Its Cover

8. Don't Bite the Hand that Feeds You

    Don't _____ the Mouth that Bites You

9. Cowboys and Indians

    Cow_____ and Indians

# Verbal Irony

Verbal irony is the use of words for the opposite of their literal meaning. If the topic of an essay is *your boring summer* an ironic title would be "My Exciting Summer."

Example: The Great Gatsby

Directions: generate your own ironic titles for the following subjects. (Remember to write the opposite of what you literally mean.)

1. Subject: A horrible near-death experience on the Colorado River

   Ironic title: A _____Lovely_____ Day on the Colorado River

2. Subject: A dentist who ruins patients' teeth

   Ironic title: The _____est Dentist in the World

3. Subject: A man's series of bumbled dates with the woman of his dreams

   Ironic title: The _____ Operator

4. Subject: A girl who loved to swim

   Ironic title:_____

5. Subject: The most dangerous skateboard park in the world

   Ironic title:_____

6. Subject: A fat monkey that loves bananas

   Ironic title:_____

7. Subject:_____
   (Pick your own subject)

   Ironic title:_____

8. Subject:_____
   (Pick your own subject)

   Ironic title:_____

# Contrasting and Contradictory Elements

Directions: add a contrasting or contradictory element.

This ____Happy_____ Sadness (Happy is the opposite of sad.)

1. My _____ Excitement (What is the opposite of excitement?)

2. My _____ Enemy (Do enemies usually love or hate?)

3. My Most Successful _____ (What contradicts success?)

# Unlikely Combinations

My Mom Loves ____to Clean up After Me_____

4. The _____ Winter (Winter is usually cold.)

5. I Love You; Let's _____ (What would a lover not want?)

6. The Sun and _____

7. The Dog and the_____
(Pick something not associated with dogs.)

8. Three Cows in _____
(Pick a place where cows do not usually go.)

9. Arctic _____
(Pick something not associated with the Arctic.)

10. Snowboarding in the _____
(Pick a place that snowboarders would not go.)

Printed in the United States
62306LVS00001BB/319-336